Excel
Basic Skills

Year
6
Ages
11 – 12

Mathematics

Get the Results You Want!

Damon James

Contents

Introduction

The aim of the ***Excel*** **Basic Skills Mathematics** series is to build on and reinforce students' basic skills in Mathematics. The books in the series support the requirements of Australian Curriculum Mathematics at each year level.

The ***Excel*** **Basic Skills Mathematics** series consists of seven books, one for each year level, from Kindergarten/Foundation to Year 6. The series is supported by other books in the ***Excel*** **Basic Skills** and **Advanced Skills** series.

Structure of the book

This book contains:

- thirty carefully graded double-page units of teaching and learning activities.
  - **Unit A** covers most of the **Number and Algebra** strands of the syllabus.
  - **Unit B** covers the rest of the **Number and Algebra** strands as well as the remaining **Measurement, Space, Statistics and Probability** strands.
- four double-page **revision units**.
- four four-page **NAPLAN-style tests**.

How to use this book

- Students should complete one unit per week. A suggested plan would be to complete the Unit A page for the week on one day and the Unit B page on another day of the same week.
- At the end of a sequence of units students should undertake the applicable Revision units. If students find particular revision questions difficult they should revisit those areas in the previous sequence of units.
- After appropriate revision activities students should undertake the NAPLAN-style Test for those units. The revision work and testing should be completed on different days.

How to use this book with the *Excel* Basic Skills English series

For a complete **weekly English and Mathematics program** use this book in conjunction with the ***Excel*** **Basic Skills English Year 6** book. This way a student will have work set for four days a week—two days for English and two days for Mathematics.

How to assess students' progress

- The results of the work undertaken in each unit can be recorded on the marking grids. The marking grids on pages 6 and 7 (please see the example on page 4) are an easy-to-use diagnostic tool that indicates where students' strengths and weaknesses lie in relation to specific areas of Mathematics. These results can be used to gather extra information about students' progress and their further revision needs.

The *Excel* Basic Skills and Advanced Skills series

If students are experiencing difficulty, require additional practice or need extension in any area of the course, further books are available to support them in the ***Excel*** **Basic Skills** and **Advanced Skills** series. (Please see the comprehensive list of ***Excel*** books on page 5.)

The *Excel* step-by-step improvement plan

Step 1

Read the introduction on page 3.

Step 2

Read this page, along with the marking grids on pages 6 and 7.

- **Unit A and B marking grids**
  The results of the work undertaken in each unit can be recorded on the marking grids.
  These are an easy-to-use diagnostic tool that indicates where each student's strengths and weaknesses are in relation to specific areas of Mathematics.
  These results can be used to gather extra information about each student's progress and their further revision needs.
  For example, see the sample marking grid below.
- If a student is consistently getting more than one in five questions wrong in any topic, they need help in this area.
- When marking answers on the grid, simply mark incorrect answers with 'X' in the appropriate box. This will result in a graphical representation of areas needing further work. An example has been done below for the first five units. If a question has several parts, it should be counted as wrong if one or more mistakes are made.
- Remember you can identify what topics a student is having difficulty with by the number of questions they get wrong. For example, in the grid below the student is having difficulty with multiplication questions.

	Addition	Subtraction	Multiplication	Multiplication	Division	Division	Addition	Addition	Subtraction	Subtraction	Multiplication	Multiplication	Division	Division	Place Value	Number Properties	Money	Money	Decimals	Decimals	Rounding	Patterns and Algebra
Question	1	2	3	4	5	6	7	8	9	10	11	12	13	14	15	16	17	18	19	20	21	22
Unit 1											X											
Unit 2												X										
Unit 3												X										
Unit 4											X	X										
Unit 5											↑	↑										
Unit 6																						
Unit 7																						
Revision 1																						
Unit 8																						
Unit 9																						
Unit 10																						

This grid indicates that the student needs extra help and practice in multiplication questions.

Step 3

Refer to page 5: ***Excel* books to help you *get the results you want!***

- Under each topic there is a comprehensive list of books in our range to help a student.
  For example, if a student wants help with multiplication questions, the books shown below will help them.
  Each ***Excel*** book has a comprehensive contents page that will identify the appropriate pages in the book to target the specific topic area that is causing problems.

Multiplication and Division

Excel **Basic Skills**

9781741251838

9781864412895

Excel **Basic Skills Core**

9781864412772

Excel **Advanced Skills**

9781741252644

Excel **NAPLAN-style Tests**

9781741254167

9781741253887

9781741254259

Excel books to help you *get the results you want!*

Number and Algebra

Place Value, Number Properties, Patterns, Algebra and Operations

Excel Basic Skills | *Excel* Basic Skills Core | *Excel* Advanced Skills | *Excel* NAPLAN-style Tests

9781741251838 | 9781864412772 | 9781741252644 | 9781741254167 | 9781741253887 | 9781741254259

Addition and Subtraction

Excel Basic Skills | *Excel* Advanced Skills | *Excel* NAPLAN-style Tests

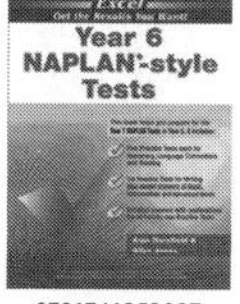

9781741251838 | 9781864412871 | 9781740200516 | 9781741252644 | 9781741254167 | 9781741253887 | 9781741254259

Multiplication and Division

Excel Basic Skills | *Excel* Basic Skills Core | *Excel* Advanced Skills | *Excel* NAPLAN-style Tests

9781741251838 | 9781864412895 | 9781864412772 | 9781741252644 | 9781741254167 | 9781741253887 | 9781741254259

Fractions, Decimals, Rounding and Money

Excel Basic Skills | *Excel* Basic Skills Core | *Excel* Advanced Skills | *Excel* NAPLAN-style Tests

9781741255904 | 9781864412901 | 9781741251838 | 9781864412772 | 9781741252644 | 9781741254167 | 9781741253887 | 9781741254259

Measurement and Space

Time and Measurement

Excel Basic Skills | *Excel* Basic Skills Core | *Excel* Advanced Skills | *Excel* NAPLAN-style Tests

9781741255904 | 9781741251838 | 9781864412772 | 9781741252644 | 9781741254167 | 9781741253887 | 9781741254259

2D/3D Shapes, Angles and Location

Excel Basic Skills | *Excel* Advanced Skills | *Excel* NAPLAN-style Tests

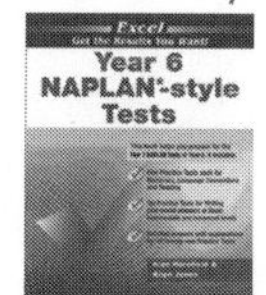

9781741251838 | 9781741252644 | 9781741254167 | 9781741253887 | 9781741254259

Statistics and Probability

Graphs, Probability and Tables/Data

Excel Basic Skills | *Excel* Advanced Skills | *Excel* NAPLAN-style Tests

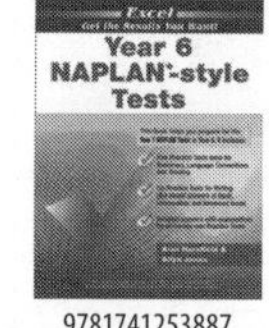

9781741251838 | 9781741252644 | 9781741254167 | 9781741253887 | 9781741254259

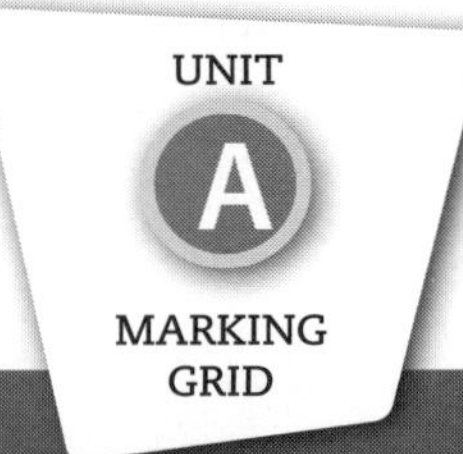

Number and Algebra

	Addition	Subtraction	Multiplication	Multiplication	Division	Division	Addition	Addition	Subtraction	Subtraction	Multiplication	Multiplication	Division	Division	Place Value	Number Properties	Money	Money	Decimals	Decimals	Rounding	Patterns and Algebra
Question	**1**	**2**	**3**	**4**	**5**	**6**	**7**	**8**	**9**	**10**	**11**	**12**	**13**	**14**	**15**	**16**	**17**	**18**	**19**	**20**	**21**	**22**
Unit 1																						
Unit 2																						
Unit 3																						
Unit 4																						
Unit 5																						
Unit 6																						
Unit 7																						
Revision 1																						
Unit 8																						
Unit 9																						
Unit 10																						
Unit 11																						
Unit 12																						
Unit 13																						
Unit 14																						
Unit 15																						
Revision 2																						
Unit 16																						
Unit 17																						
Unit 18																						
Unit 19																						
Unit 20																						
Unit 21																						
Unit 22																						
Unit 23																						
Revision 3																						
Unit 24																						
Unit 25																						
Unit 26																						
Unit 27																						
Unit 28																						
Unit 29																						
Unit 30																						
Revision 4																						
Question	**1**	**2**	**3**	**4**	**5**	**6**	**7**	**8**	**9**	**10**	**11**	**12**	**13**	**14**	**15**	**16**	**17**	**18**	**19**	**20**	**21**	**22**

UNIT B MARKING GRID

	Number and Algebra							Measurement and Space										Statistics and Probability				
	Addition	Subtraction	Multiplication	Division	Fractions	Fractions	Operations	Time	Time	Measurement—units	Measurement—length/area	Measurement—capacity/volume/mass	2D Shapes	3D Shapes	Location	Location	Angles	Probability	Probability	Tables/Data	Graphs	Graphs
Question	1	2	3	4	5	6	7	8	9	10	11	12	13	14	15	16	17	18	19	20	21	22
Unit 1																						
Unit 2																						
Unit 3																						
Unit 4																						
Unit 5																						
Unit 6																						
Unit 7																						
Revision 1																						
Unit 8																						
Unit 9																						
Unit 10																						
Unit 11																						
Unit 12																						
Unit 13																						
Unit 14																						
Unit 15																						
Revision 2																						
Unit 16																						
Unit 17																						
Unit 18																						
Unit 19																						
Unit 20																						
Unit 21																						
Unit 22																						
Unit 23																						
Revision 3																						
Unit 24																						
Unit 25																						
Unit 26																						
Unit 27																						
Unit 28																						
Unit 29																						
Unit 30																						
Revision 4																						
Question	1	2	3	4	5	6	7	8	9	10	11	12	13	14	15	16	17	18	19	20	21	22

1

+	17	16	19	14	12	15
18						

2

–	40	25	21	36	34	18
13						

3

×	6	9	3	8	2	1
5						

4

×	4	7	10	11	12	5
8						

5

÷	15	18	9	21	6	36
3						

6

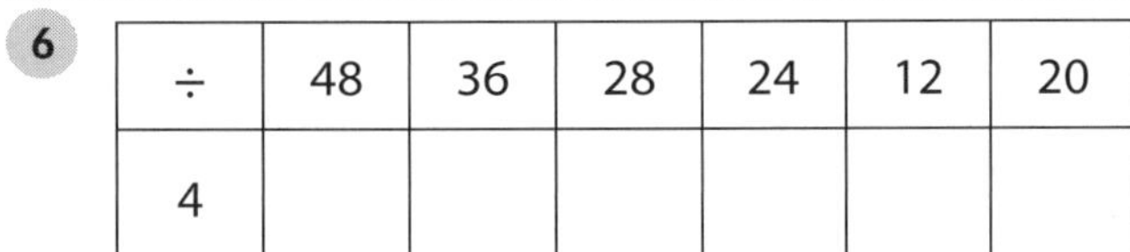

÷	48	36	28	24	12	20
4						

7

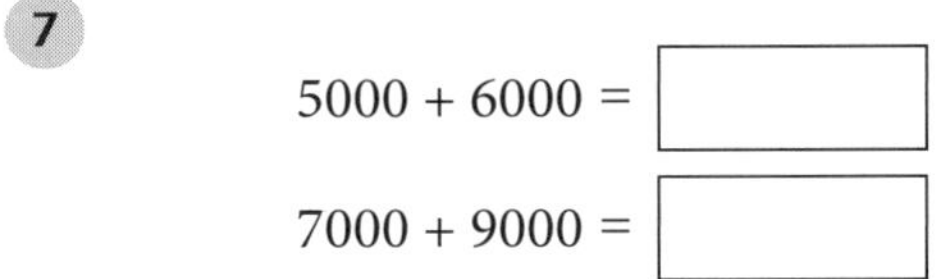

5000 + 6000 = ☐

7000 + 9000 = ☐

8

```
  12 943        14 742
+ 13 867      + 10 685
```

9

12 270 – 4160 = ☐

10 What is the difference between 26 210 and 23 081?

☐

11 What is the total number of days in 6 weeks?

☐ days

12 Find the product of ninety and sixty.

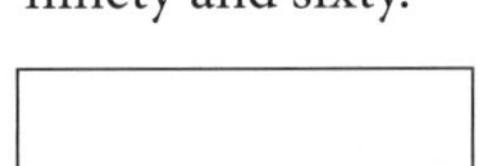

13

81 ÷ 9 = ☐

10 ÷ 10 = ☐

14 How many balls will each of 6 boys get if 24 balls are shared equally?

☐

15 Circle the largest number.

42 609 42 598 42 611 42 600

16

$3^2 =$ ☐ $9^2 =$ ☐

17 Find the total amount.

$4369 $2421 $6112 = ☐

18 Round to the nearest 50c before adding to estimate the total.

$3.26
$6.36
$4.95

☐

19 Order the decimals from smallest to largest.

8.33 8.05 8.46 8.6

☐

20 Add 6.92, 6.34 and 8.08. ☐

21 Round each number to the nearest 10.

18 407 ☐ 29 396 ☐ 71 178 ☐

22 Complete the number pattern.

3, 5, 8, 12, ☐, ☐

UNIT 1B

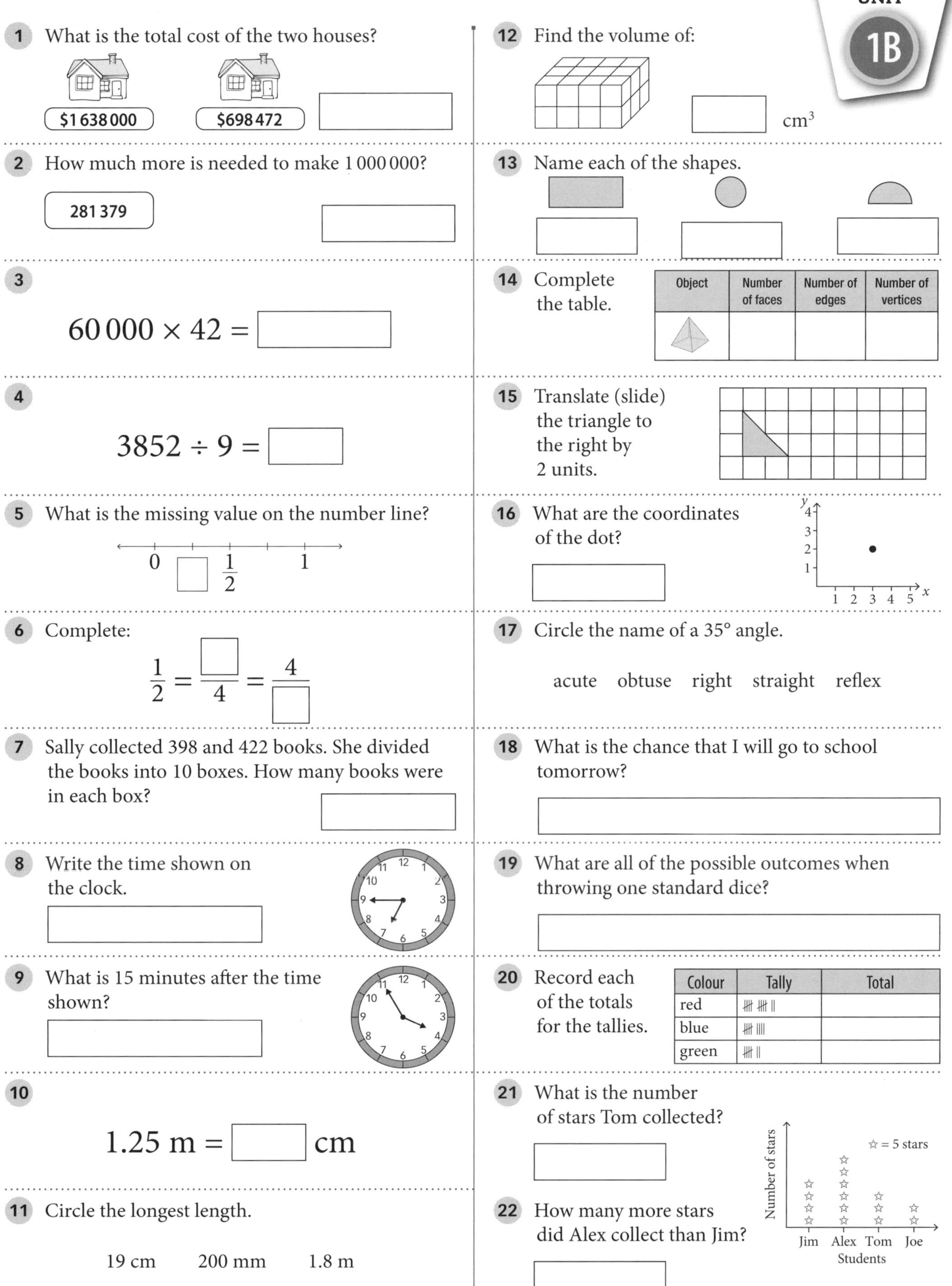

1 What is the total cost of the two houses?

$1 638 000 $698 472

2 How much more is needed to make 1 000 000?

281 379

3

$60\,000 \times 42 =$ ☐

4

$3852 \div 9 =$ ☐

5 What is the missing value on the number line?

0 ☐ $\frac{1}{2}$ 1

6 Complete:

$\frac{1}{2} = \frac{\square}{4} = \frac{4}{\square}$

7 Sally collected 398 and 422 books. She divided the books into 10 boxes. How many books were in each box?

8 Write the time shown on the clock.

9 What is 15 minutes after the time shown?

10

$1.25\text{ m} =$ ☐ cm

11 Circle the longest length.

19 cm 200 mm 1.8 m

12 Find the volume of:

☐ cm^3

13 Name each of the shapes.

14 Complete the table.

Object	Number of faces	Number of edges	Number of vertices

15 Translate (slide) the triangle to the right by 2 units.

16 What are the coordinates of the dot?

17 Circle the name of a 35° angle.

acute obtuse right straight reflex

18 What is the chance that I will go to school tomorrow?

19 What are all of the possible outcomes when throwing one standard dice?

20 Record each of the totals for the tallies.

Colour	Tally	Total
red	𝍸 𝍸 ‖	
blue	𝍸 ‖‖	
green	𝍸 ‖	

21 What is the number of stars Tom collected?

22 How many more stars did Alex collect than Jim?

1

+	23	14	19	6	25	28
17						

2

–	50	35	43	19	31	46
15						

3

×	6	4	9	8	5	3
5						

4

×	2	10	7	12	11	9
8						

5

÷	36	24	27	18	6	33
3						

6

÷	16	44	24	28	8	48
4						

7

9000 + 8000 = ☐

2000 + 11 000 = ☐

8

  46 326
+ 18 919

  22 645
+ 10 732

9

17 360 – 12 210 = ☐

10 What is the difference between 27 426 and 18 179?

☐

11 What is the total number of days in 4 weeks?

☐ days

12 Find the product of twenty and seventy.

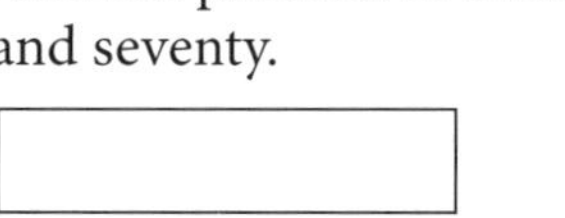

13

72 ÷ 9 = ☐

56 ÷ 7 = ☐

14 How many books will each of 3 girls get if 18 books are shared equally?

☐

15 Circle the largest number.

92 721 92 790 92 709 92 127

16

$7^2 =$ ☐ $4^2 =$ ☐

17 Find the total amount.

$7108 $2395 $8465 = ☐

18 Round to the nearest 50c before adding to estimate the total.

$7.10
$8.55
$7.63

☐

19 Order the decimals from smallest to largest.

9.63 9.05 9.2 9.37

☐

20 Add 2.476, 3.911 and 4.850. ☐

21 Round each number to the nearest 10.

73 888 ☐ 24 791 ☐ 96 424 ☐

22 Complete the number pattern.

8, 16, 24, 32, ☐, ☐

UNIT 2B

1 What is the total cost of the two houses?

$689 428 $479 386

2 How much more is needed to make 1 000 000?

117 985

3

$80\,000 \times 56 =$ ☐

4

$71\,648 \div 8 =$ ☐

5 What is the missing value on the number line?

0 ☐ $\frac{1}{4}$ $\frac{1}{2}$

6 Complete:

$\frac{1}{3} = \frac{\square}{6} = \frac{3}{\square}$

7 Joe was given $55 and earned $110. He donated $63 to charity. How much money did Joe have left?

8 Write the time shown on the clock.

9 What is 15 minutes after the time shown?

10

9.3 cm = ☐ mm

11 Circle the longest length.

12 mm 1.3 cm 0.4 m

12 Find the volume of:

☐ cm^3

13 Name each of the shapes.

14 Complete the table.

Object	Number of faces	Number of edges	Number of vertices

15 Translate (slide) the triangle up by 1 unit.

16 What are the coordinates of the square?

17 Circle the name of a 235° angle.

acute obtuse right straight reflex

18 What is the chance that I will go to the movies tomorrow?

19 What are all of the possible outcomes when spinning this spinner?

6 1 4 2

20 Record each of the totals for the tallies.

Size	Tally	Total
small	𝍸 𝍸 𝍸 𝍸	
medium	𝍸 𝍸 𝍸 |	
large	𝍸 𝍸 𝍸 |||	

21 How many newspapers were delivered on Wednesday?

22 What was the total number of newspapers delivered for the week?

= 10 newspapers

Number of papers

M T W Th. F

Days

1

+	27	19	10	14	25	36
19						

2

−	24	41	47	23	36	50
12						

3

×	4	12	9	1	10	6
5						

4

×	2	7	11	3	8	5
8						

5

÷	9	12	21	18	30	3
3						

6

÷	16	44	28	4	36	20
4						

7

4000 + 7000 = ☐

12 000 + 9000 = ☐

8

$$\begin{array}{r} 72\,721 \\ +\ 41\,335 \\ \hline \end{array} \qquad \begin{array}{r} 98\,544 \\ +\ 11\,627 \\ \hline \end{array}$$

9

13 590 − 4110 = ☐

10 What is the difference between 27 274 and 31 965?

11 What is the total number of days in 7 weeks?

☐ days

12 Find the product of eighty and sixty.

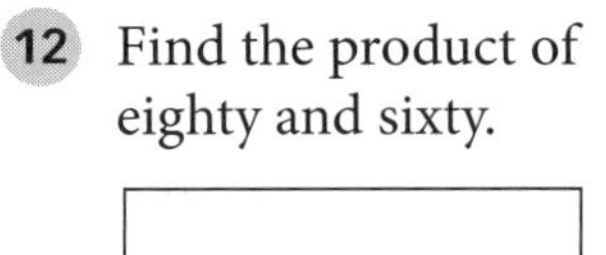

13

36 ÷ 9 = ☐

24 ÷ 3 = ☐

14 How many toys will each of 5 puppies get if 20 toys are shared equally?

15 Circle the largest number.

111 063   116 013   116 310   113 106

16

$2^2 =$ ☐ $10^2 =$ ☐

17 Find the total amount.

= ☐

18 Round to the nearest 50c before adding to estimate the total.

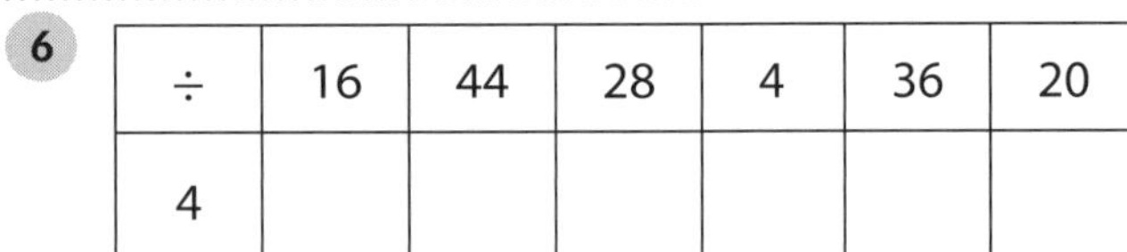

19 Order the decimals from smallest to largest.

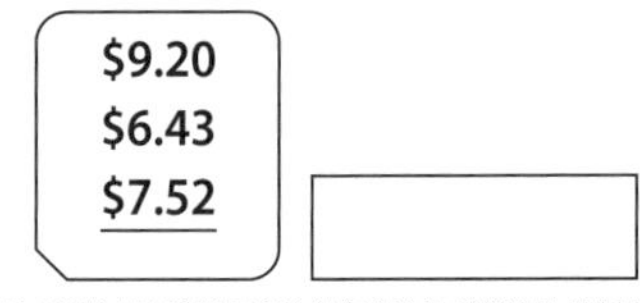

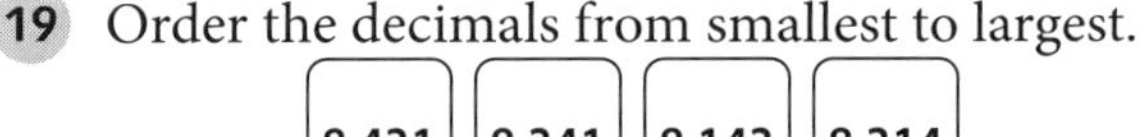

20 Add 1.83, 9.76 and 8.54.

21 Round each number to the nearest 10.

41 489 ☐   26 243 ☐   11 107 ☐

22 Complete the number pattern.

96, 107, 118, ☐, ☐

UNIT **3B**

1 What is the total cost of the two houses?

$947 836 $1 428 900

2 How much more is needed to make 1 000 000?

876 392

3

$40\,000 \times 83 =$ ☐

4

$5352 \div 6 =$ ☐

5 What is the missing value in:

$\frac{1}{10}, \frac{1}{9}, \frac{☐}{☐}, \frac{1}{7}$?

6 Complete:

$\frac{☐}{12} = \frac{☐}{8} = \frac{1}{4}$

7 Zoe picked 1000 flowers. She was also given 500 flowers. She sold 750 flowers. How many flowers did Zoe have left?

8 Write the time shown on the clock.

9 What is 30 minutes after the time shown?

10

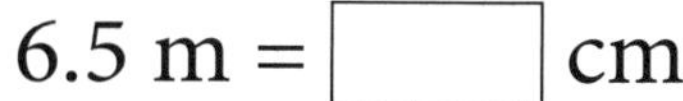

6.5 m = ☐ cm

11 Circle the longest length.

90 cm 0.85 m 800 mm

12 Find the volume of:

☐ cm^3

13 Name each of the shapes.

14 Complete the table.

Object	Number of faces	Number of edges	Number of vertices

15 Translate (slide) the diamond to the left by 1 unit.

16 What are the coordinates of the square?

17 Circle the name of a 180° angle.

acute obtuse right straight reflex

18 What is the chance that I will go on a plane next week?

19 What are all of the possible outcomes of selecting from this set of cards?

4 7 9 3 4

20 Record each of the totals for the tallies.

Drink	Tally	Total
water	卌 卌 卌 卌 |||	
juice	卌 卌 |||	
tea	卌 卌 卌		
coffee	卌 卌 卌 卌 卌 卌		

21 What is the number of boxes delivered in Week 2?

22 Which week had the most boxes delivered?

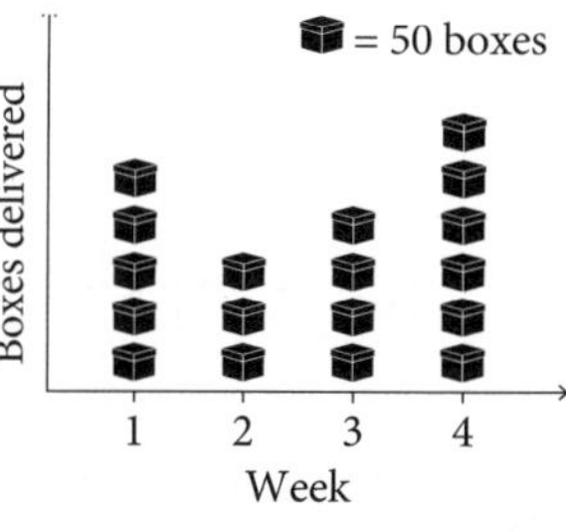

1

+	26	29	15	8	19	35
13						

2

−	31	50	22	37	47	39
18						

3

×	3	11	8	10	4	9
5						

4

×	2	6	0	12	7	5
8						

5

÷	9	33	15	24	6	27
3						

6

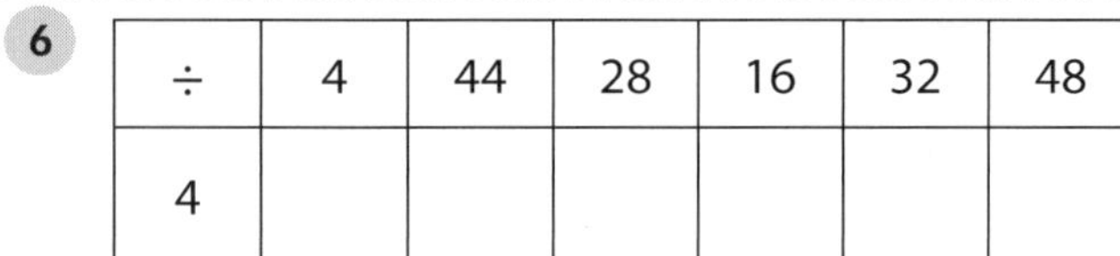

÷	4	44	28	16	32	48
4						

7

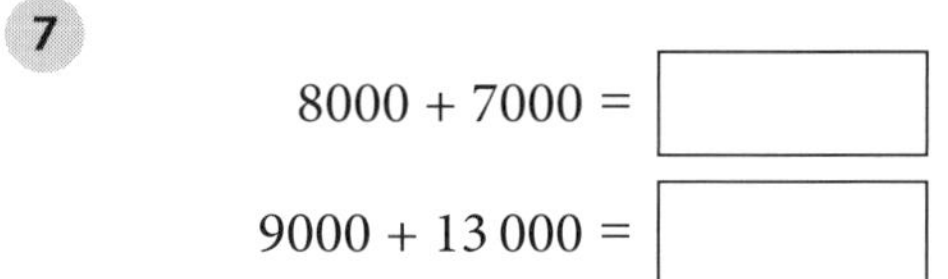

8000 + 7000 = ☐

9000 + 13 000 = ☐

8

  32 521
+ 76 835

  49 754
+ 62 163

9

27 837 + 14 427 = ☐

10 What is the difference between 36 690 and 21 450?

☐

11 What is the total number of days in 9 weeks?

☐ days

12 Find the product of forty and zero.

☐

13

42 ÷ 7 = ☐

108 ÷ 9 = ☐

14 How many balls will each of 6 tubs get if 72 balls are shared equally?

☐

15 Circle the largest number.

279 146   276 419   274 916   279 503

16

$1^2 =$ ☐ $5^2 =$ ☐

17 Find the total amount.

$1555 $2321 $4652   = ☐

18 Round to the nearest 50c before adding to estimate the total.

$10.56
$9.30
$7.85

☐

19 Order the decimals from smallest to largest.

6.308   6.083   6.038   6.803

☐

20 Add 7.66, 8.93 and 6.581.

☐

21 Round each number to the nearest 10.

91 012 ☐   26 367 ☐   91 198 ☐

22 Complete the number pattern.

32, 42, 62, 92, ☐, ☐

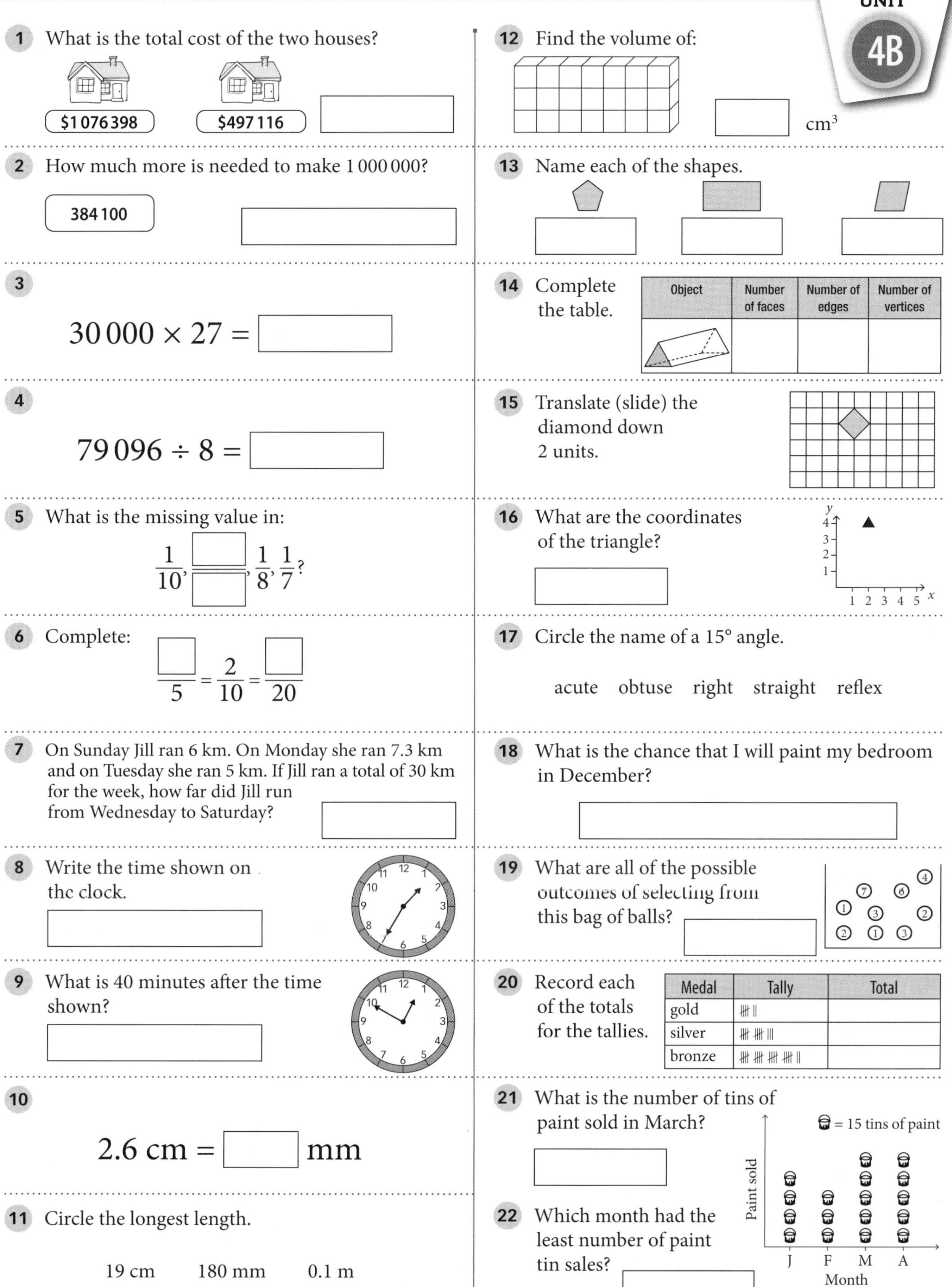

1 What is the total cost of the two houses?

$1 076 398 $497 116

2 How much more is needed to make 1 000 000?

384 100

3

$30\,000 \times 27 =$

4

$79\,096 \div 8 =$

5 What is the missing value in:

$\frac{1}{10}, \frac{\square}{\square}, \frac{1}{8}, \frac{1}{7}?$

6 Complete:

$\frac{\square}{5} = \frac{2}{10} = \frac{\square}{20}$

7 On Sunday Jill ran 6 km. On Monday she ran 7.3 km and on Tuesday she ran 5 km. If Jill ran a total of 30 km for the week, how far did Jill run from Wednesday to Saturday?

8 Write the time shown on the clock.

9 What is 40 minutes after the time shown?

10

2.6 cm = ☐ mm

11 Circle the longest length.

19 cm 180 mm 0.1 m

12 Find the volume of:

cm^3

13 Name each of the shapes.

14 Complete the table.

Object	Number of faces	Number of edges	Number of vertices

15 Translate (slide) the diamond down 2 units.

16 What are the coordinates of the triangle?

17 Circle the name of a 15° angle.

acute obtuse right straight reflex

18 What is the chance that I will paint my bedroom in December?

19 What are all of the possible outcomes of selecting from this bag of balls?

20 Record each of the totals for the tallies.

Medal	Tally	Total
gold	卌 ॥	
silver	卌 卌 |||	
bronze	卌 卌 卌 卌 ॥	

21 What is the number of tins of paint sold in March?

22 Which month had the least number of paint tin sales?

1

+	29	7	27	35	42	18
16						

2

–	19	50	21	36	24	47
17						

3

×	9	4	2	8	5	11
5						

4

×	7	3	10	12	1	6
8						

5

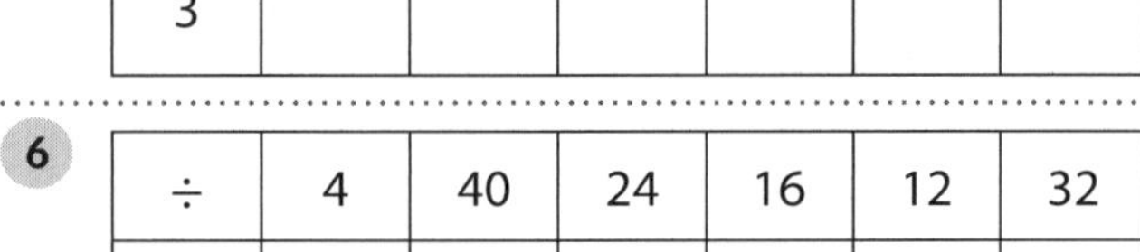

÷	6	24	27	18	30	3
3						

6

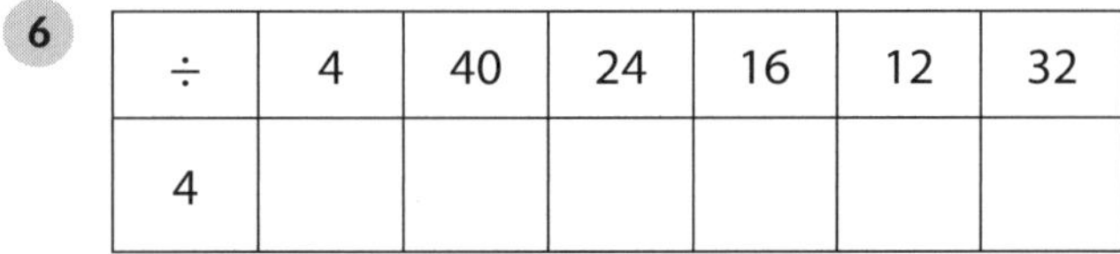

÷	4	40	24	16	12	32
4						

7

6000 + 3000 = ☐

8000 + 11 000 = ☐

8

$$\begin{array}{r} 47\,385 \\ +\ 29\,117 \\ \hline \end{array} \qquad \begin{array}{r} 77\,424 \\ +\ 11\,636 \\ \hline \end{array}$$

9

14 992 + 21 437 = ☐

10 What is the difference between 64 810 and 15 580?

☐

11 What is the total number of days in 10 weeks?

☐ days

12 Find the product of thirty and seventy.

☐

13

72 ÷ 6 = ☐

32 ÷ 4 = ☐

14 How many marbles will each of 10 bags get if 100 marbles are shared equally?

☐

15 Circle the largest number.

107 216 102 167 107 039 106 785

16

$6^2 =$ ☐ $8^2 =$ ☐

17 Find the total amount.

$6321 $3476 $7895 = ☐

18 Round to the nearest 50c before adding to estimate the total.

$7.66
$9.05
$4.19

☐

19 Order the decimals from smallest to largest.

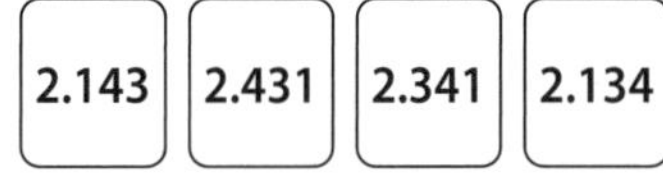

☐

20 Add 3.614, 8.729 and 4.117. ☐

21 Round each number to the nearest 10.

17 647 ☐ 99 853 ☐ 27 116 ☐

22 Complete the number pattern.

71, 76, 82, 89, ☐, ☐

UNIT 5B

1 What is the total cost of the two houses?

$893 855 $960 421

2 How much more is needed to make 1 000 000?

732 185

3 $400\,000 \times 63 =$ ☐

4 $23\,688 \div 3 =$ ☐

5 What is the missing value on the number line?

0 ☐ $\frac{1}{3}$

6 Complete:

$\frac{\square}{6} = \frac{4}{12} = \frac{\square}{24}$

7 Jack was collecting cans to recycle. In Week 1 he collected 251 cans. In Week 2 he collected 365 cans. Jack's target was 1000 cans. How many cans did Jack need to collect in Week 3 to reach his target?

8 Write the time shown on the clock.

9 What is 25 minutes after the time shown?

10 45 cm = ☐ mm

11 Circle the longest length.

120 cm 1.6 m 1000 mm

12 Find the volume of:

☐ cm^3

13 Name each of the shapes.

14 Complete the table.

Object	Number of faces	Number of edges	Number of vertices

15 Translate (slide) the triangle 2 units to the right.

16 What are the coordinates of the star?

17 Circle the name of a 195° angle.

acute obtuse right straight reflex

18 What is the chance that I will go swimming tomorrow?

19 What are all of the possible outcomes of selecting a diamond card from a standard pack of cards?

20 Record each of the totals for the tallies.

Clothing	Tally	Total
T-shirt	𝍸 𝍸 𝍸 𝍸 ‖	
shorts	𝍸 𝍸 |||	
jumper	𝍸 𝍸 ||||	
hat	|||	

21 What is the number of cans collected in Week 1?

22 Which week was the most number of cans collected?

= 50 cans

Cans collected

Week

1 2 3 4

1

+	21	16	27	8	18	30
24						

2

−	26	41	29	37	46	50
19						

3

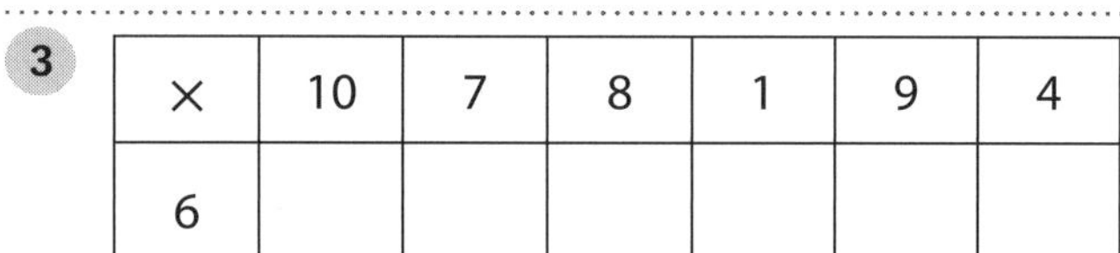

×	10	7	8	1	9	4
6						

4

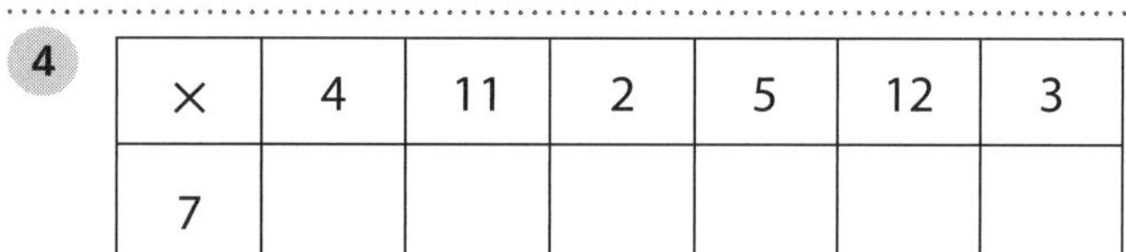

×	4	11	2	5	12	3
7						

5

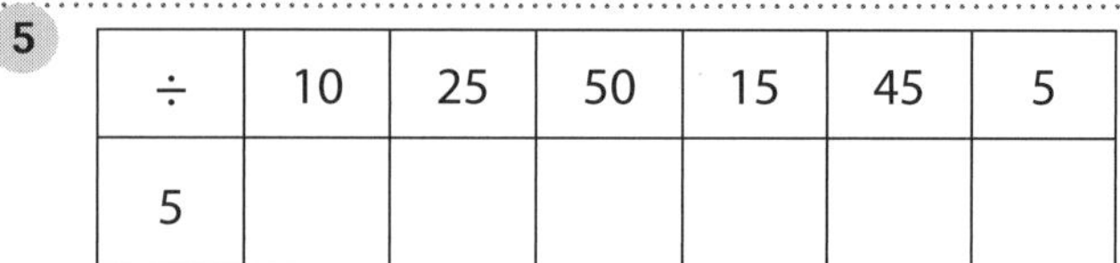

÷	10	25	50	15	45	5
5						

6

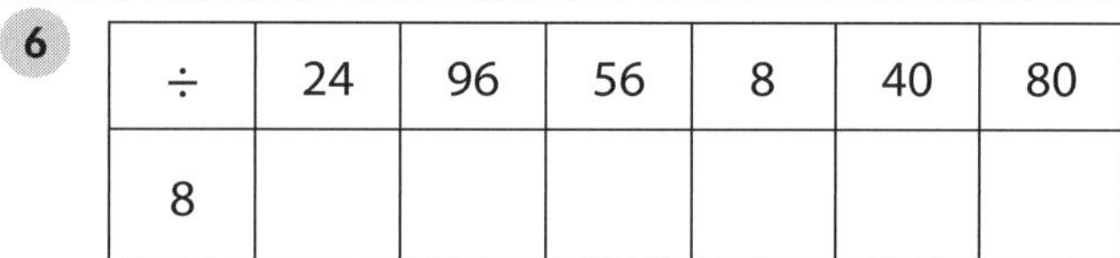

÷	24	96	56	8	40	80
8						

7

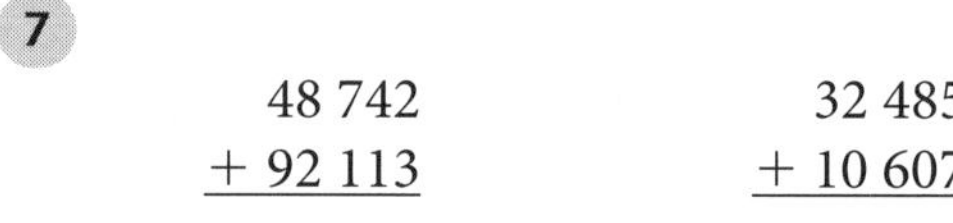

$$\begin{array}{r} 48\,742 \\ +\ 92\,113 \\ \hline \end{array} \qquad \begin{array}{r} 32\,485 \\ +\ 10\,607 \\ \hline \end{array}$$

8 Find the sum of 70 000 and 80 000.

9 How much more is needed to make 7000 from 5210?

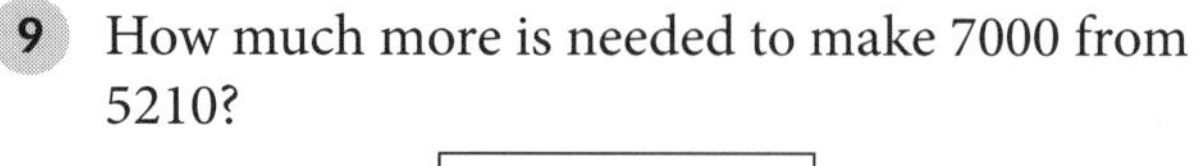

10 Use the number line to show 151 – 85 = ☐

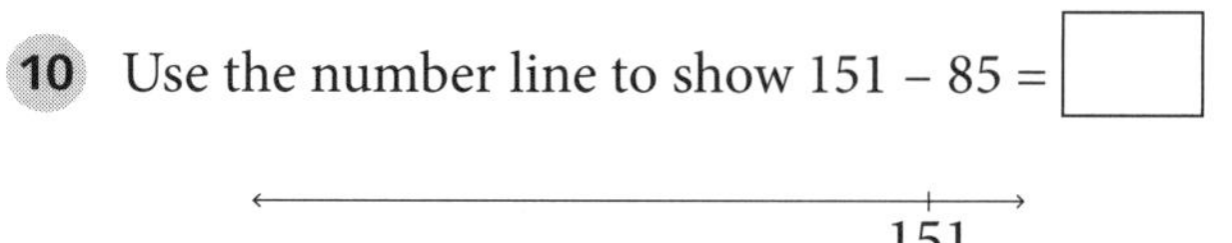

11

$$\begin{array}{r} 40 \\ \times\ \ 7 \\ \hline \end{array} \qquad \begin{array}{r} 50 \\ \times\ \ 6 \\ \hline \end{array}$$

12 Find the total cost of 10 hats at $80 each.

13

$$20 \div 6 = \square$$

14

$$4\overline{)88}$$

15 True or false? 2 is a prime number.

16 Order the numbers from smallest to largest.

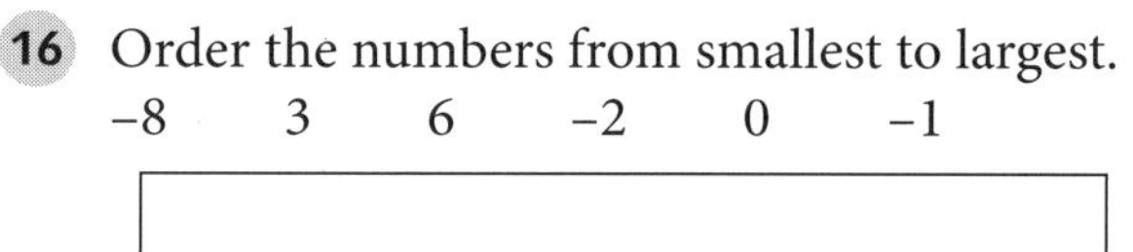

−8 3 6 −2 0 −1

17 Find the change from $900.

18 Round to the nearest $1 before adding to estimate.

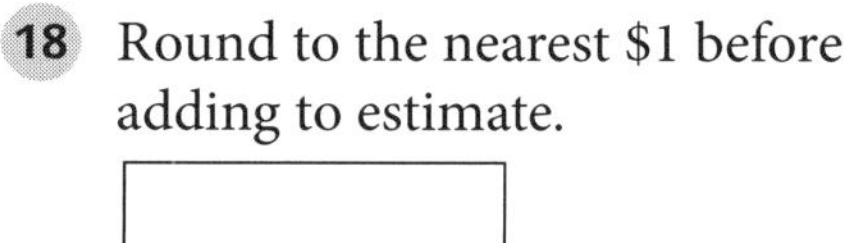

$13.95
$10.60
$ 8.15

19 Find the difference between 6.03 and 7.91.

20 Colour the largest number.

3.216 3.4 3.083 3.096

21 Round each number to the nearest hundred.

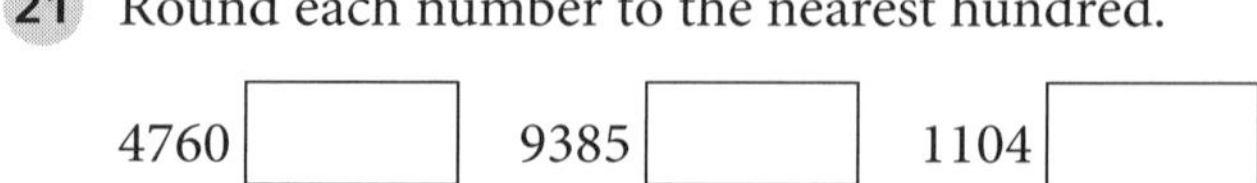

4760 ☐ 9385 ☐ 1104 ☐

22 Complete the number pattern.

1, 3, 9, ☐, ☐, ☐

1 Find the total of 32 106, 93 188 and 24 637.

2 What is the difference between the values on the two cards?

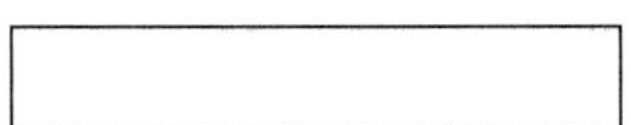

3 What is 29 groups of 3286?

4 $60\,000 \div 8 =$ ☐

5 $\frac{1}{2} + \frac{1}{4} =$ ☐

6 Complete the number line.

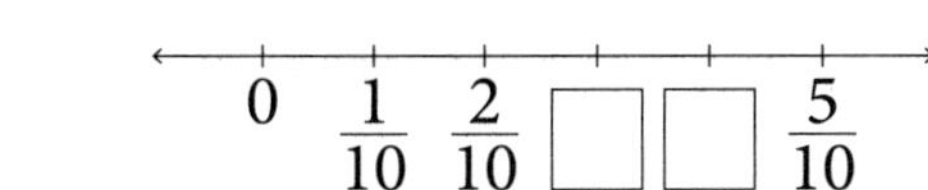

7 $6 + (3 \times 2) - 9 =$ ☐

8 Draw 9:40 on the clock.

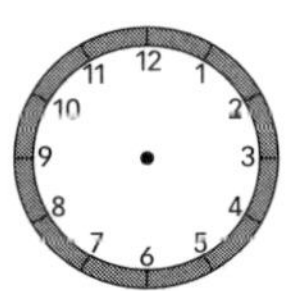

9 Convert 13:00 to am/pm time.

10 $1.25\text{ m} + 25\text{ cm} =$ ☐

11 Find the perimeter.

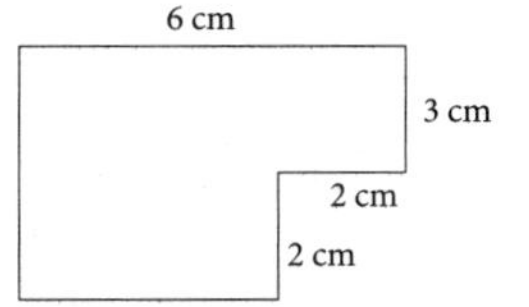

12 Circle the greatest volume.

13 Circle the shape that is **not** a triangle.

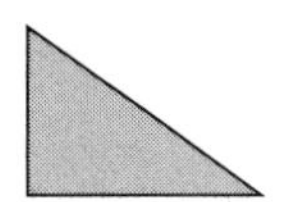
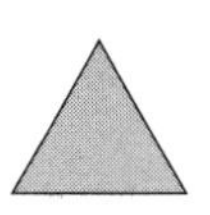
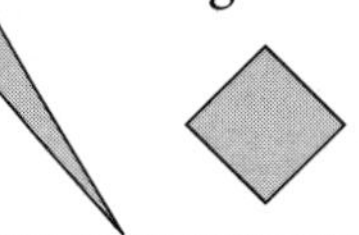
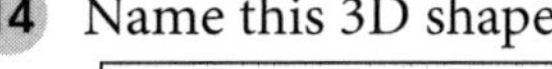
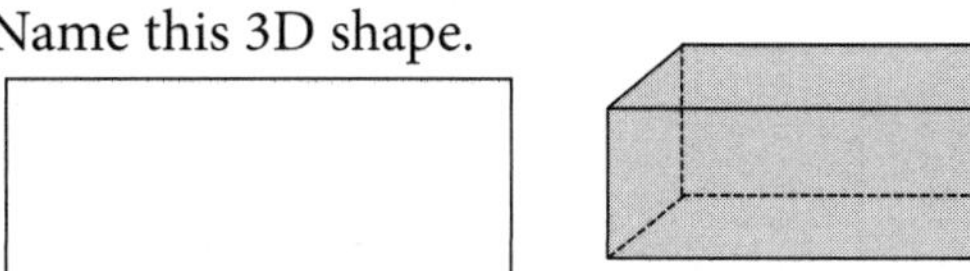

14 Name this 3D shape.

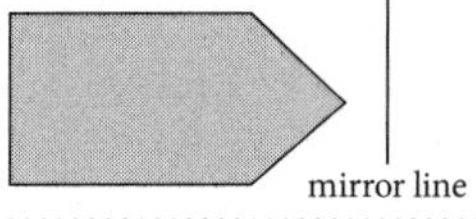

15 Reflect the shape about the mirror line.

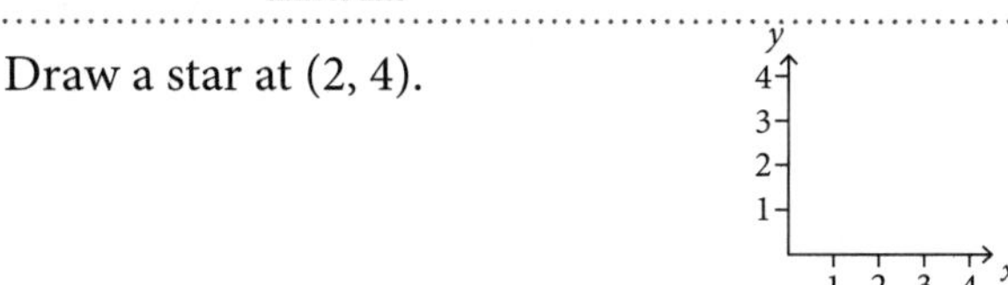

16 Draw a star at (2, 4).

17 Estimate the size of this angle.

☐ °

18 What is the chance (as a fraction) that a red ball will be selected from the box?

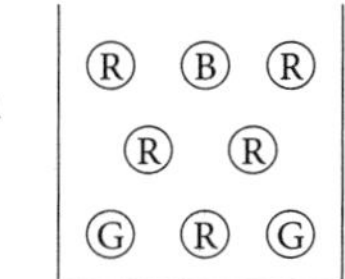

19 Circle the spinner that has a $\frac{1}{4}$ chance of green being selected.

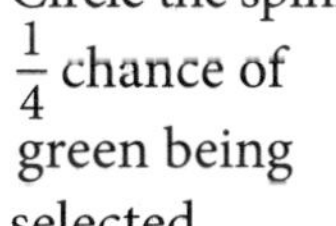

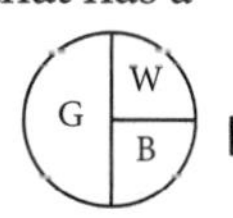

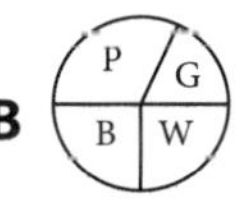

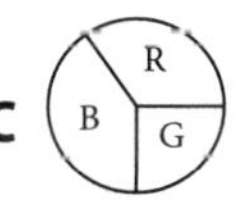

20 How many more apples than pears were eaten?

Fruit	Number eaten
apple	41
banana	52
pear	27
peach	14
apricot	26

21 How many trees were sold in June?

22 Add the sale of 700 trees for September to the graph.

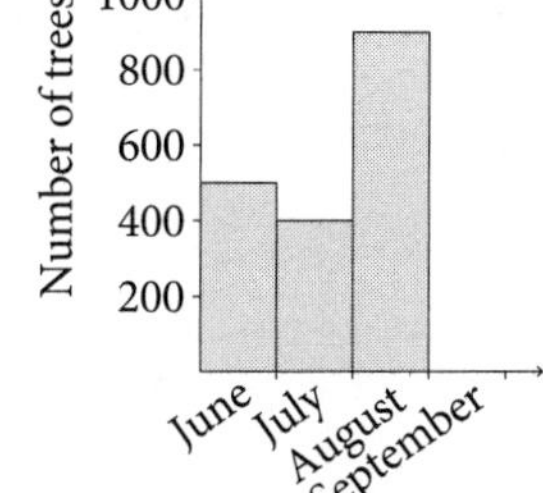

1

+	29	7	18	31	25	11
23						

2

–	41	33	19	49	25	38
16						

3

×	7	1	4	11	8	3
6						

4

×	2	6	10	5	12	9
7						

5

÷	30	15	60	45	5	55
5						

6

÷	24	48	8	88	72	32
8						

7

  39 245
+ 84 131

  63 562
+ 17 515

8 Find the sum of 200 000 and 900 000.

9 How much more is needed to make 90 000 from 26 005?

10 Use the number line to show 162 – 76 = ☐

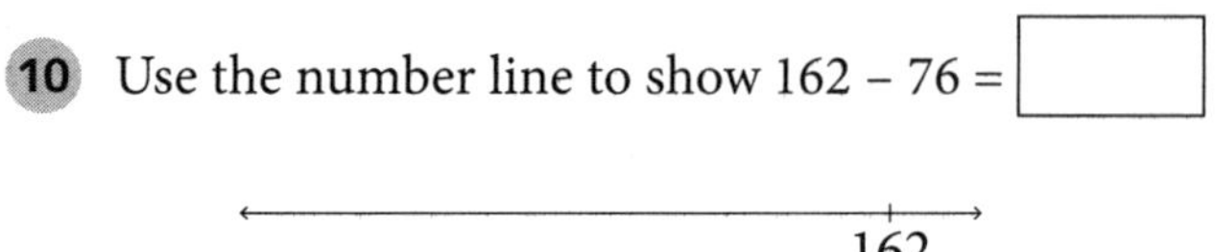

11

  30
× 9

  60
× 5

12 Find the total cost of 3 bags of apples at \$20 each bag.

$20.00

13

$30 \div 7 =$ ☐

14

3) 99

15 True or false? 5 is a prime number.

16 Order the numbers from smallest to largest.

7 −8 −4 2 0 1

17 Find the change from \$900.

$179

18 Round to the nearest \$1 before adding to estimate.

$17.66
$18.02
$ 9.90

19 Find the difference between 7.26 and 5.89.

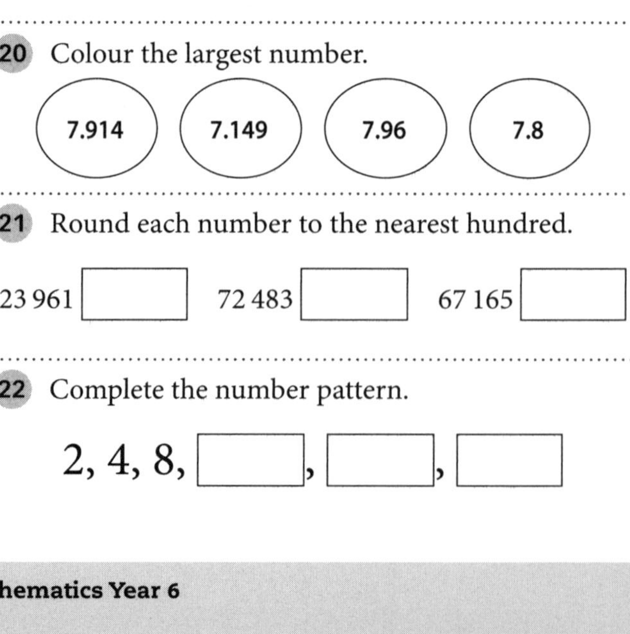

20 Colour the largest number.

7.914 7.149 7.96 7.8

21 Round each number to the nearest hundred.

23 961 ☐ 72 483 ☐ 67 165 ☐

22 Complete the number pattern.

2, 4, 8, ☐, ☐, ☐

1 Find the total of 42 986, 107 385 and 69 117.

2 What is the difference between the values on the two cards?

89 763 | 400 301

3 What is 85 groups of 4683?

4 $70\,000 \div 9 =$

5 $\frac{1}{4} + \frac{3}{8} =$

6 Complete the number line.

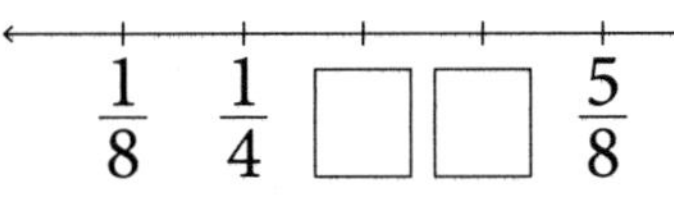

7 $3 \times (100 \div 10) - 25 =$

8 Draw 1:05 on the clock.

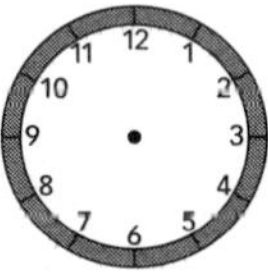

9 Convert 23:15 to am/pm time.

10 $31\text{ cm} + 25\text{ mm} =$

11 Find the perimeter.

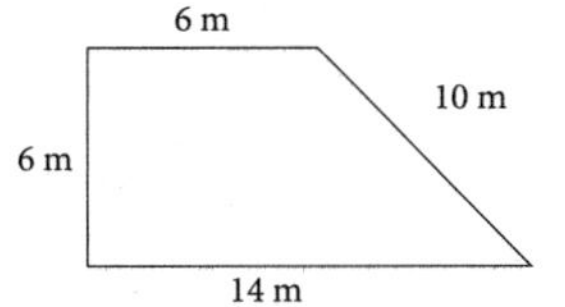

12 Circle the greatest volume.

9000 mL

13 Circle the shape that is **not** a rectangle.

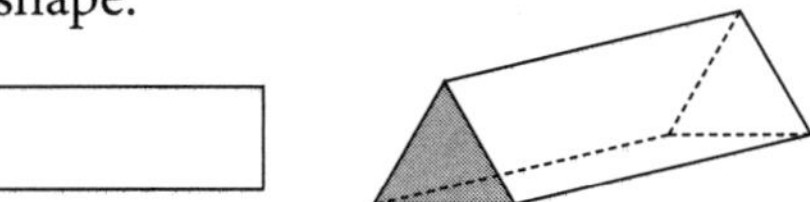

14 Name this 3D shape.

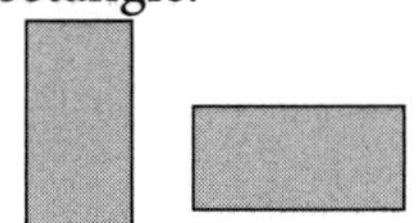

15 Reflect the shape about the mirror line.

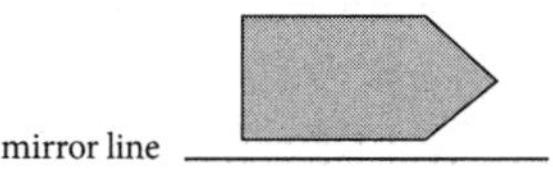

16 Draw a circle at (3, 2).

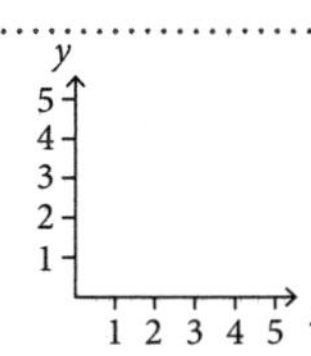

17 Estimate the size of this angle.

18 What is the chance (as a fraction) that a card with the number 3 will be selected?

1 | 4 | 3 | 2 | 6 | 3 | 1 | 3

19 Circle the spinner that has a $\frac{1}{3}$ chance of red being selected.

A 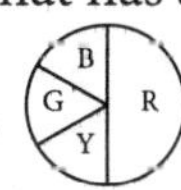

B 

C 

20 How many more bottles of water were sold than bottles of juice?

Drink	Number sold
milk	20
apple juice	15
orange juice	17
soft drink	37
water	63

21 How many bikes were sold in February?

22 Add the sale of 250 bikes in April to the graph.

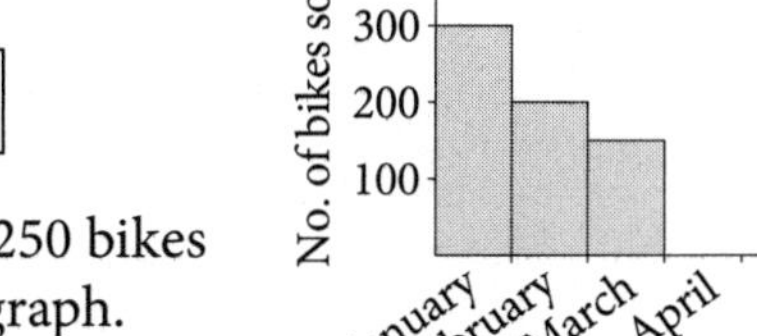

1

+	26	17	9	29	14	10
18						

2

–	40	21	18	37	26	33
13						

3

×	1	6	4	7	10	12
5						

4

×	8	2	9	11	3	5
8						

5

÷	36	27	15	9	21	3
3						

6

÷	36	16	8	32	20	12
4						

7 $9000 + 8000 =$ ☐

8

$$\begin{array}{r} 32\,146 \\ +\ 46\,937 \\ \hline \end{array}$$

A 79 083 **B** 68 083 **C** 78 083 **D** 69 073

9 $32\,420 - 18\,180 =$ ☐

10 What is the difference between 97 378 and 4196?

11

$$\begin{array}{r} 30 \\ \times\ \ 9 \\ \hline \end{array}$$

A 120 **B** 180 **C** 270 **D** 360

12 Find the product of eleven and ninety.

13 What is

$40 \div 7$? ☐

14 How many books will each of 3 students get if 24 books are shared equally?

15 Select the largest number.

A 246 789 **B** 247 685
C 247 865 **D** 248 675

16

$9^2 =$ ☐

17 Find the total amount of the three cards.

$305 $620 $245

18 Round to the nearest 50c before adding to estimate the total.

$$\begin{array}{r} \$6.20 \\ \$3.90 \\ +\ \$4.45 \\ \hline \end{array}$$

19 Find the difference between 7.36 and 5.83.

20 Add 3.24, 1.06 and 7.934.

Is the answer greater than 12? ☐

21 Round 64 965 to the nearest hundred.

22 Complete the number pattern.

8, 16, 24, ☐, ☐, ☐

1 What is the total cost of the two cars?

$56 300 $49 800

2 How much more is needed to make $1 000 000?

$369 411

3 What is 40 000 × 15?

4 $8000 \div 8 =$ ☐

5 $\frac{1}{4} + \frac{2}{8} =$ ☐

6 Complete the number line.

0 $\frac{1}{4}$ ☐ 1

7 $(60 \div 5) \div 4 =$ ☐

8 Draw 9:35 on the clock.

9 What is the time 40 minutes after the time shown?

10 4.9 cm = ☐ mm

11 Which is the longest length?

A 21 cm
B 2200 mm
C 0.2 m

12 Find the volume.

☐ cm^3

13 What is the name of the shape?

A parallelogram **B** trapezium
C pentagon **D** hexagon

14 How many edges does this shape have?

15 Reflect the shape about the mirror line.

A **B**
C **D**

mirror line

16 What are the coordinates of the circle?

17 What is the name of a 230° angle?

A acute **B** obtuse
C straight **D** reflex

18 What is the chance of selecting a red ball from the bag?

R B G R R B R G

19 What are all of the possible outcomes of the cards?

1 3 4 7 4

20 What is the total of the tally?

卌 卌 ||

The graph shows the number of boxes mailed in the first four months of the year.

Number: 200, 150, 100, 50
Month: January, February, March, April

21 How many boxes were mailed in January?

22 What was the difference between the number of boxes mailed in January and April?

1 Alex has two cards.
What is the total of the two cards?

A 90 900
B 91 900
C 100 900
D 101 900

32 500	69 400

2 Chan finds the difference between 71 310 and 63 180. What is his answer?

A 8130
B 8230
C 8270
D 8490

3 To find the product of eight and sixteen, you need to

A add.
B subtract.
C multiply.
D divide.

4 What is the remainder when 50 is divided by 3?

A 1
B 2
C 3
D 4

5 Jill wins the game if she chooses the largest number. Which number should she select?

A 716 985
B 717 031
C 71 799
D 717 100

6 Which card has the largest value?

A	B	C	D
8^2	7×7	9×2	$10 + 10$

7 Two pieces of wood are measured.
What is the difference in lengths of the wood?

A 4.03 m
B 4.33 m
C 5.23 m
D 7.41 m

8 7965 rounded to the nearest hundred is

A 8000.
B 7100.
C 7900.
D 7970.

9 Sophie is solving a puzzle which is a pattern. What is the next number in the pattern?

9, 18, 27, ☐

10 A company wants to earn \$1 000 000. They have made \$325 689 so far this year. How much more money do they need to earn to reach \$1 000 000?

A \$674 311
B \$685 311
C \$774 421
D \$785 421

11 What is the missing number on the number line?

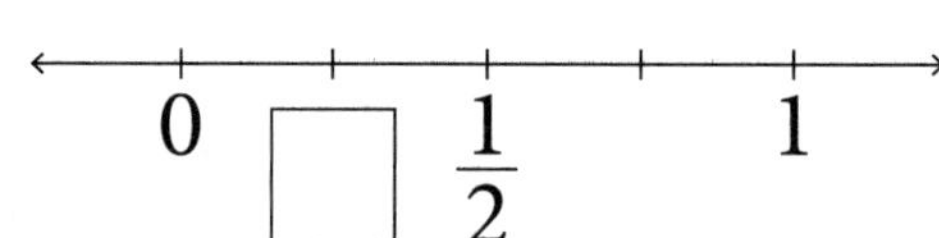

12 School starts at . The first class, spelling, goes for 50 minutes. What time does spelling class finish?

A 8:50
B 9:30
C 9:40
D 9:50

13 Dan is converting centimetres to millimetres. What is 10.6 cm in millimetres?

A 1.06 mm
B 10.06 mm
C 106 mm
D 1060 mm

14 Emma wants to build this object. She needs to know how many cubes are required. What is the number of cubes?

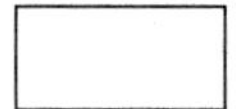

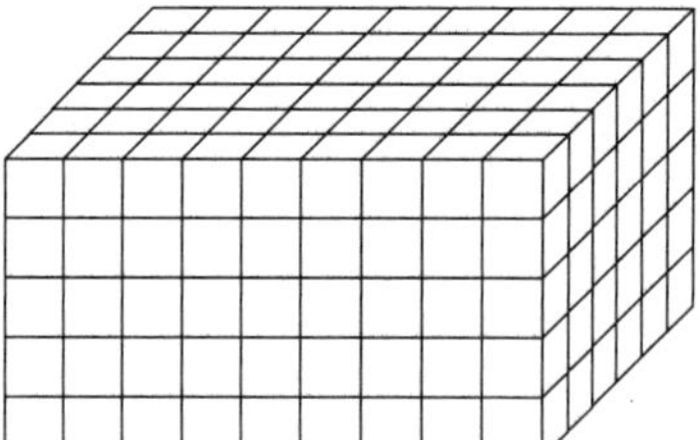

15 What is this shape reflected in the mirror line?

A 

B

C 

D

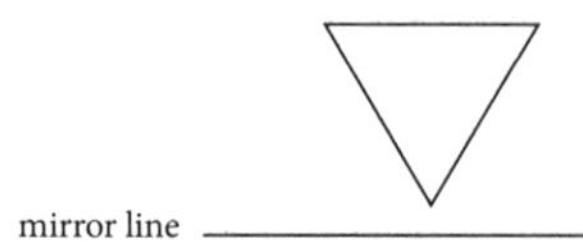

16 What are the coordinates of Point C?

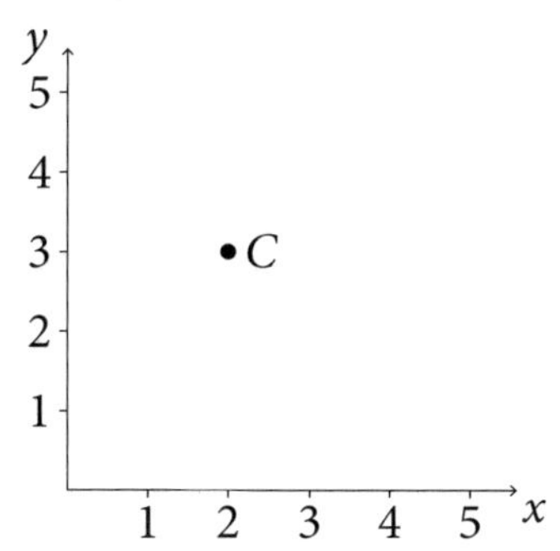

A (1, 2)
B (3, 1)
C (3, 2)
D (2, 3)

17 How many edges does a triangular prism have?

A 5
B 6
C 8
D 9

18 What is the name of this angle?

A obtuse
B acute
C reflex
D full revolution

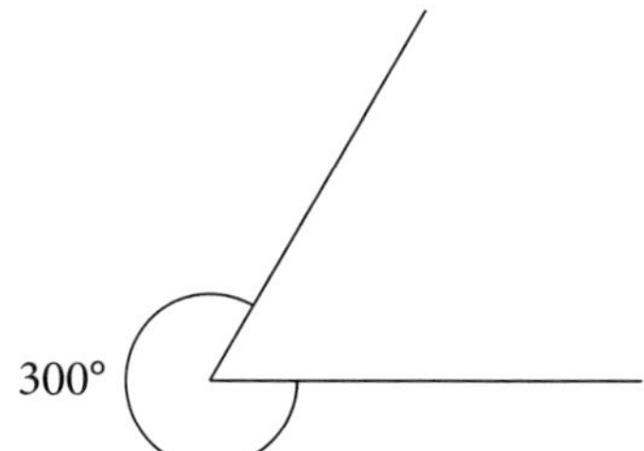

19 This is the net of a dice.

What are all the possible outcomes when rolling the dice?

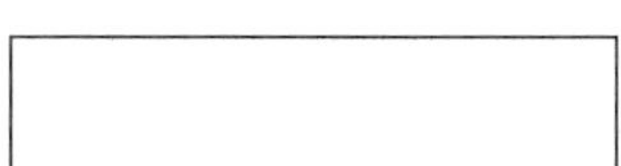

		8	
2	4	6	12
		10	

20 The number of envelopes mailed was recorded for 4 weeks.

What was the difference between the number of envelopes mailed in Weeks 2 and 4?

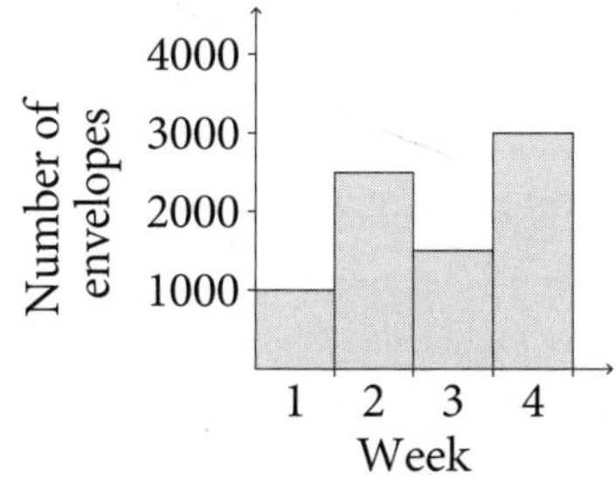

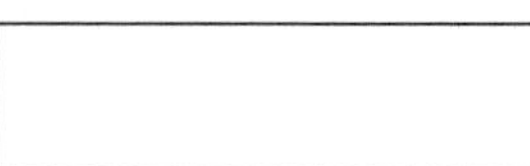

UNIT **8A**

1

+	7	12	18	27	21	9
25						

2

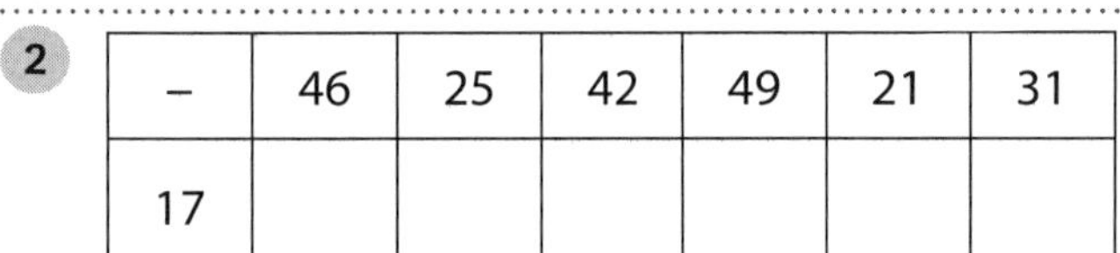

−	46	25	42	49	21	31
17						

3

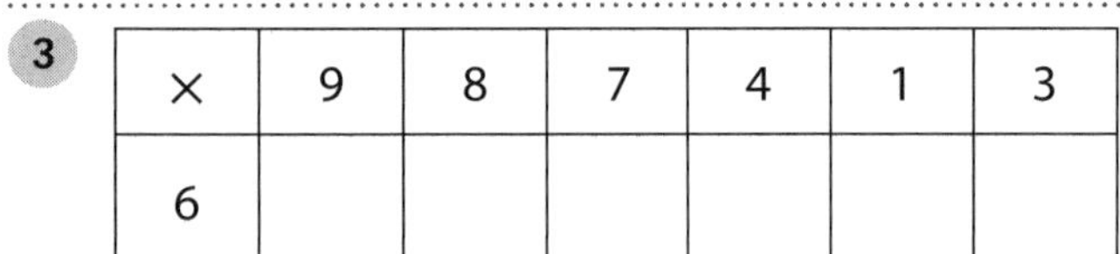

×	9	8	7	4	1	3
6						

4

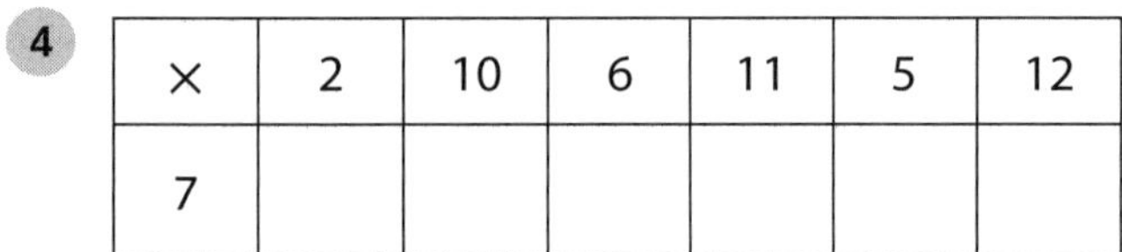

×	2	10	6	11	5	12
7						

5

÷	60	5	40	30	15	55
5						

6

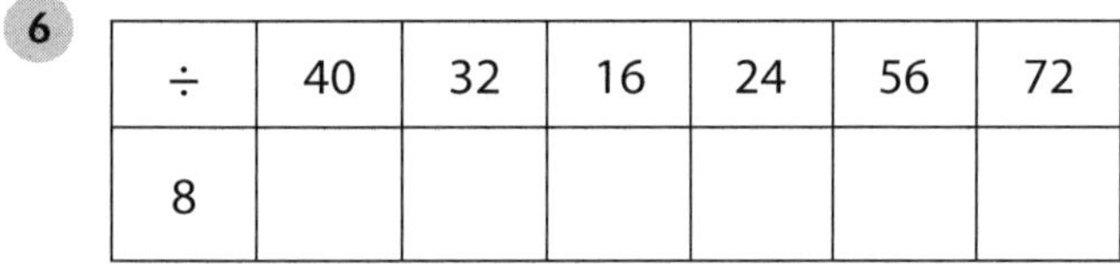

÷	40	32	16	24	56	72
8						

7

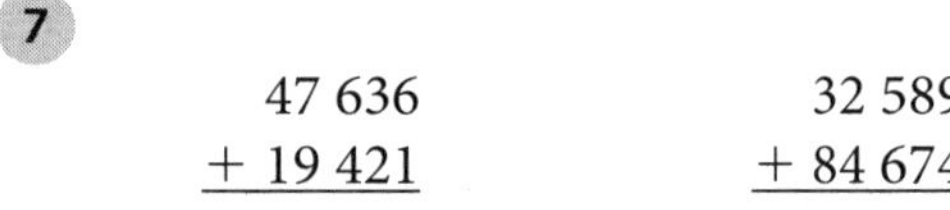

$$\begin{array}{r} 47\,636 \\ +\ 19\,421 \\ \hline \end{array} \qquad \begin{array}{r} 32\,589 \\ +\ 84\,674 \\ \hline \end{array}$$

8 Find the sum of 300 000 and 800 000.

9 How much more is needed to make 10 000 from 1709?

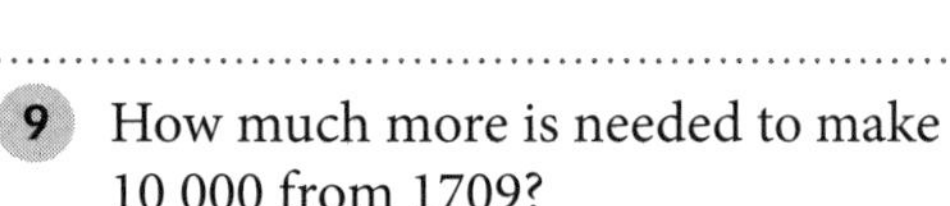

10 Use the number line to show 195 − 127 = ☐

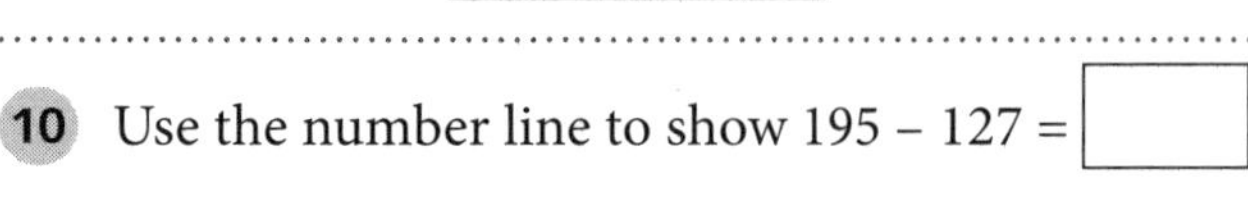

11

$$\begin{array}{r} 20 \\ \times\ \ 7 \\ \hline \end{array} \qquad \begin{array}{r} 40 \\ \times\ \ 9 \\ \hline \end{array}$$

12 Find the total cost of 70 books at $9 each.

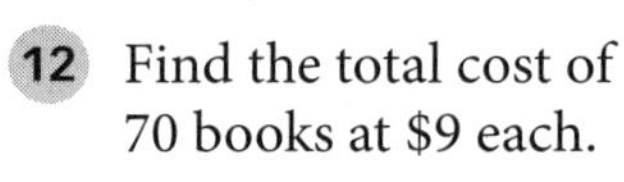

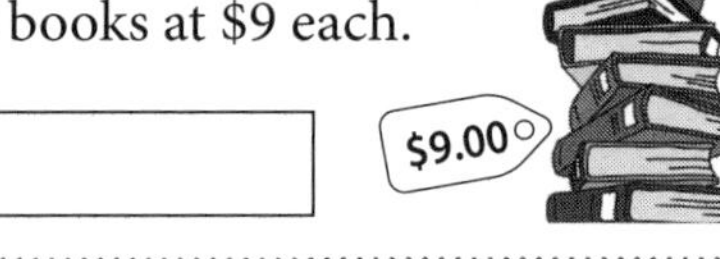

13

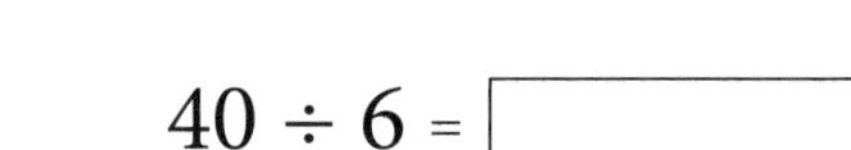

$40 \div 6 =$ ☐

14

$3\overline{)63}$

15 True or false? 9 is a prime number.

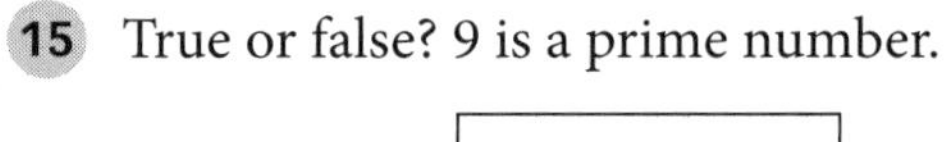

16 Order the numbers from smallest to largest.

−9 3 −8 7 6 1

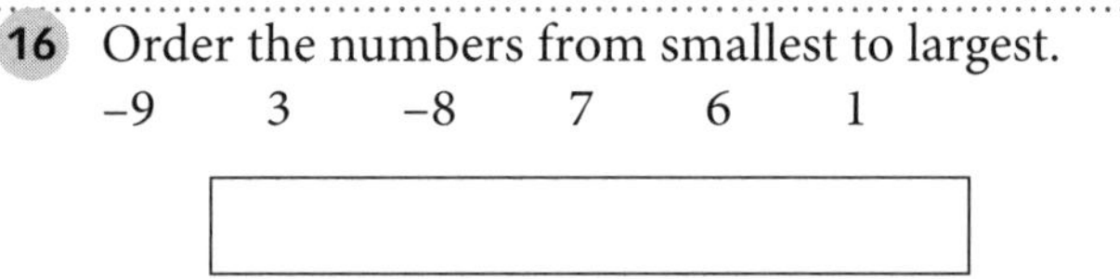

17 Find the change from $900.

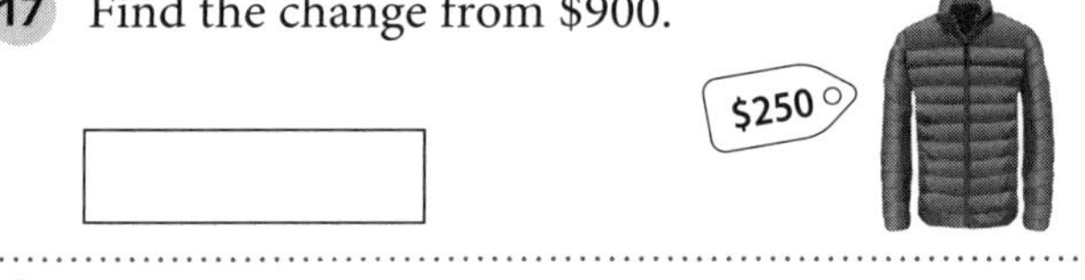

18 Round to the nearest $1 before adding to estimate.

$ 3.96
$ 8.25
$11.90

19 Find the difference between 1.09 and 3.96.

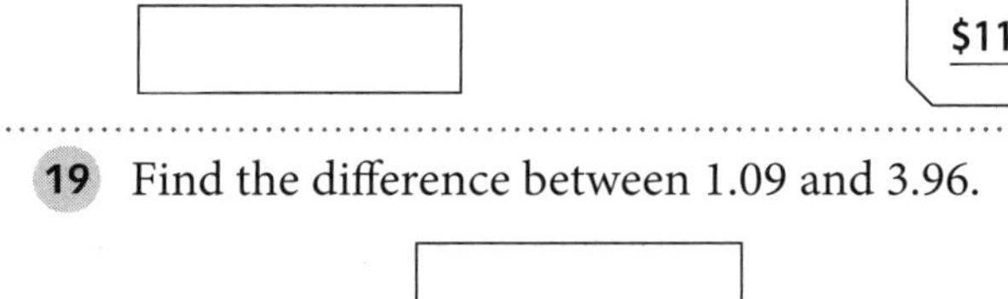

20 Colour the largest number.

21 Round each number to the nearest hundred.

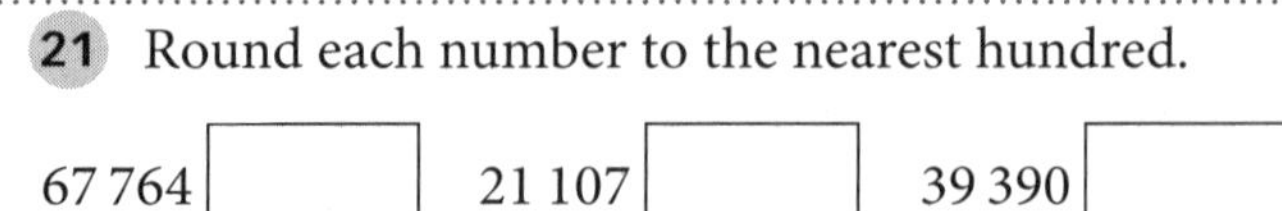

67 764 ☐ 21 107 ☐ 39 390 ☐

22 Complete the number pattern.

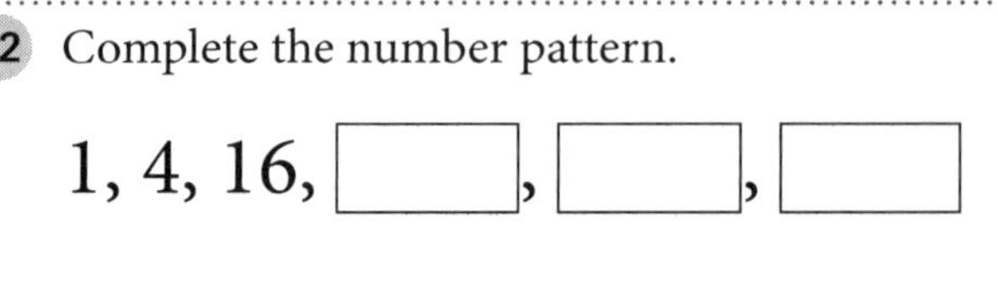

1, 4, 16, ☐, ☐, ☐

1 Find the total of 92 784, 116 349 and 284 107.

2 What is the difference between the values on the two cards?

90 046 | 107 948

3 What is 72 groups of 7381?

4 $80\,000 \div 5 =$

5 $\frac{1}{3} + \frac{1}{2} =$

6 Complete the number line.

0 $\frac{1}{4}$ ☐ ☐ 1

7 $6 \times (80 - 10) + 14 =$

8 Draw 7:55 on the clock.

9 Convert 15:30 to am/pm time.

10 $9.7 \text{ m} + 50 \text{ cm} =$

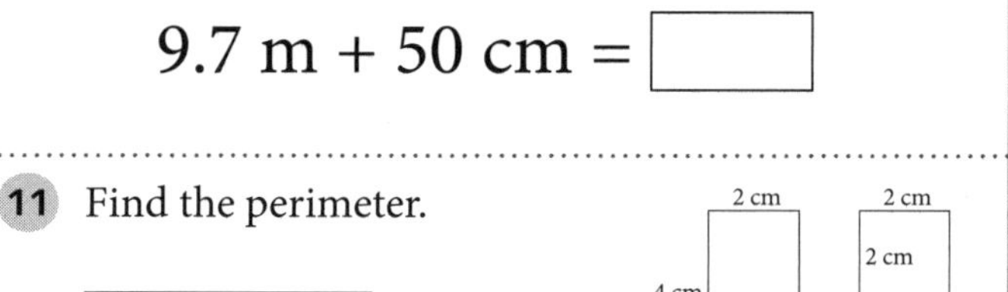

11 Find the perimeter.

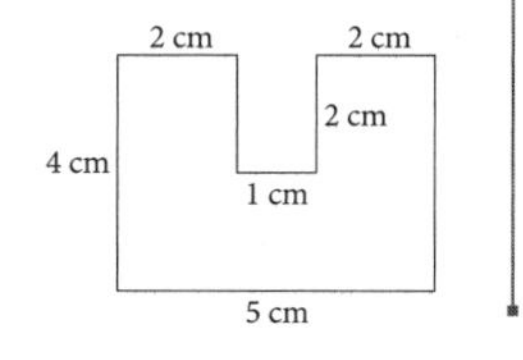

12 Circle the greatest volume.

6500 mL 6.3 L

13 Circle the shape that is **not** a circle.

14 Name this 3D shape.

15 Reflect the shape about the mirror line.

mirror line

16 Draw a square at (1, 5).

17 Estimate the size of this angle.

°

18 What is the chance (as a fraction) that a red pencil will be selected?

RED GREEN BLUE GREEN RED BLUE YELLOW RED BLACK PINK

19 Circle the spinner that has a $\frac{2}{5}$ chance of red being selected.

A B C

20 How many more hats were sold than sunglasses?

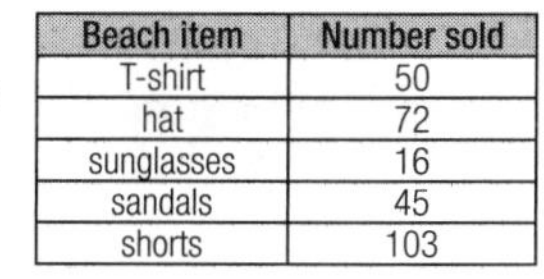

Beach item	Number sold
T-shirt	50
hat	72
sunglasses	16
sandals	45
shorts	103

21 How many starfish were counted at the beach?

22 Add 39 seagulls to the graph.

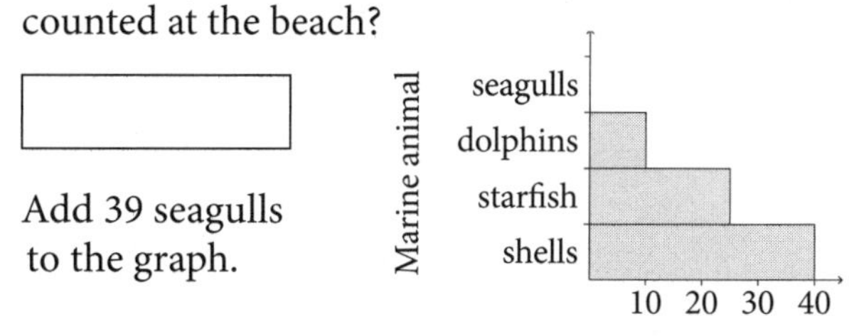

1

+	19	6	27	17	23	38
21						

2

–	40	28	51	20	47	31
18						

3

×	4	3	9	10	12	1
6						

4

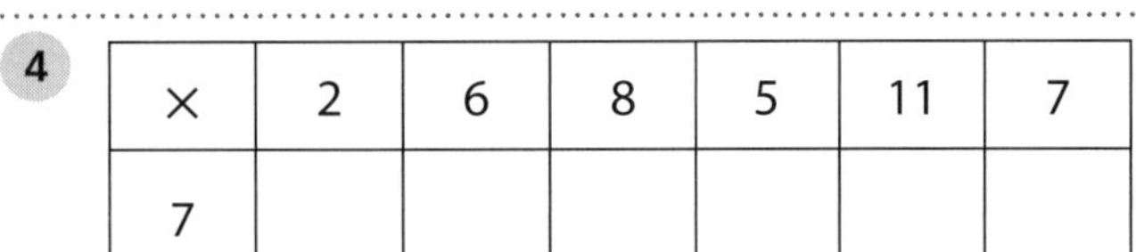

×	2	6	8	5	11	7
7						

5

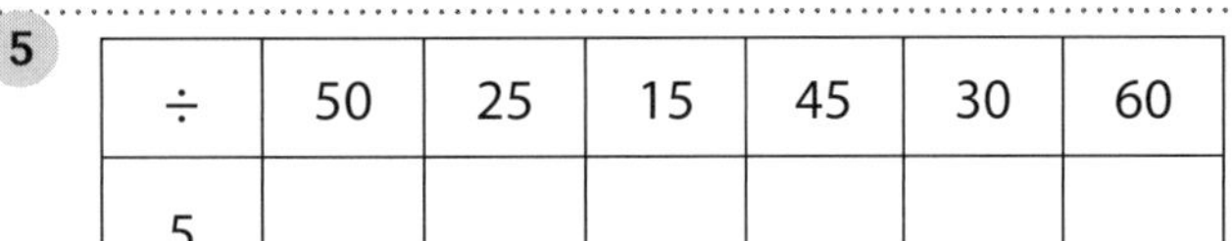

÷	50	25	15	45	30	60
5						

6

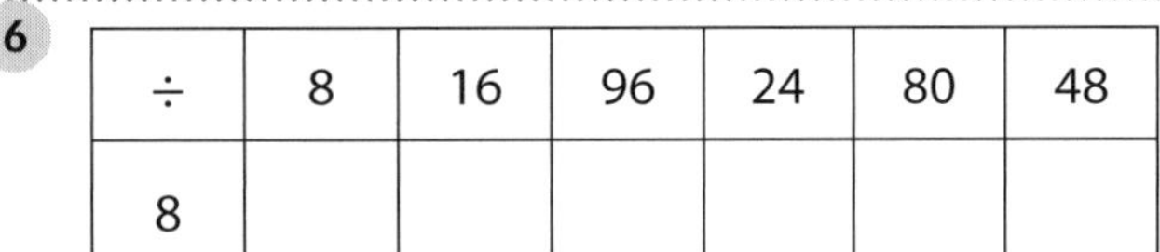
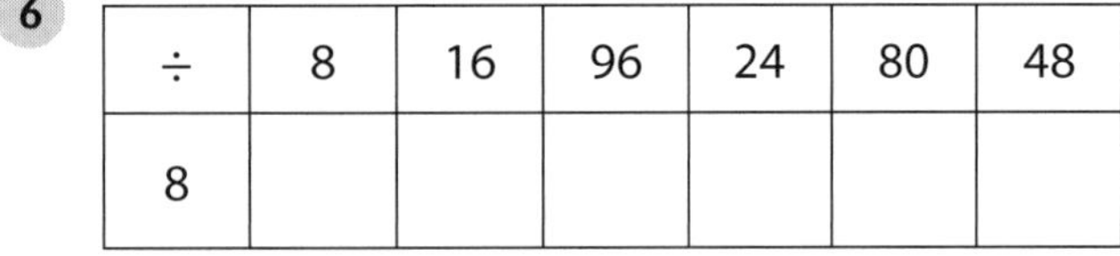

÷	8	16	96	24	80	48
8						

7

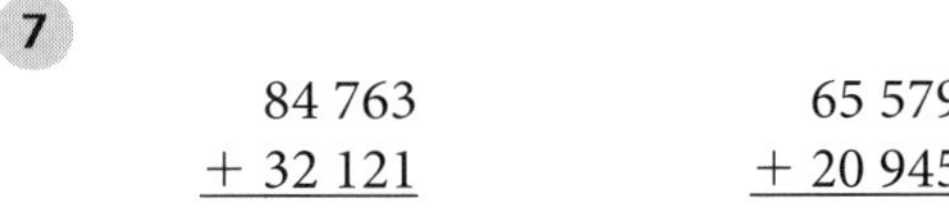

$$\begin{array}{r} 84\,763 \\ +\ 32\,121 \\ \hline \end{array} \qquad \begin{array}{r} 65\,579 \\ +\ 20\,945 \\ \hline \end{array}$$

8 Find the sum of 80 000 and 90 000.

9 How much more is needed to make 20 000 from 7908?

10 Use the number line to show 137 – 65 = ☐

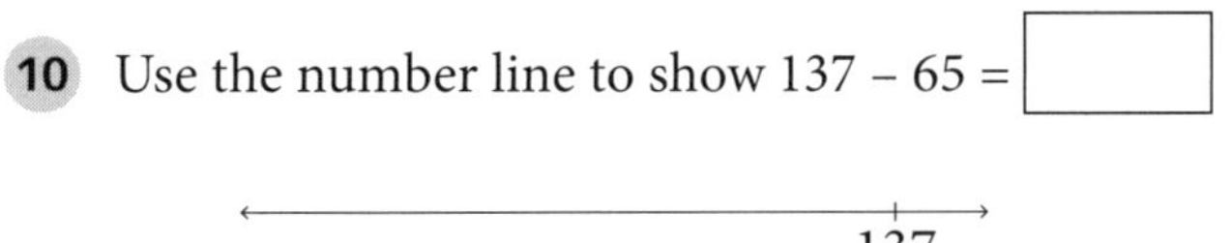

11

$$\begin{array}{r} 40 \\ \times\ \ 7 \\ \hline \end{array} \qquad \begin{array}{r} 80 \\ \times\ \ 3 \\ \hline \end{array}$$

12 Find the total cost of 50 drinks at $3 each.

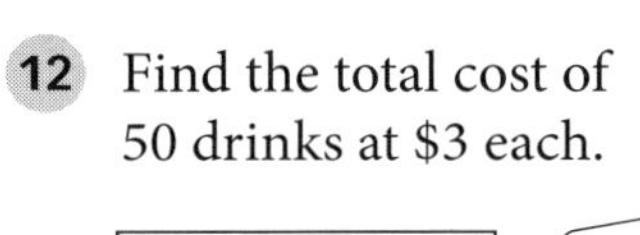

13

$50 \div 8 =$ ☐

14

$5\overline{)510}$

15 True or false? 11 is a prime number.

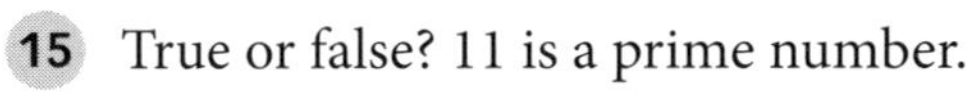

16 Order the numbers from smallest to largest.

2 8 –4 –2 0 6 1

17 Find the change from $900.

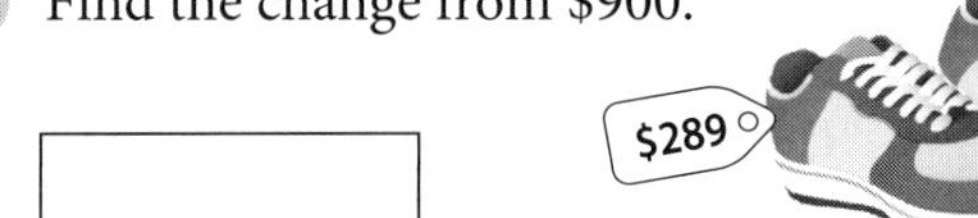

18 Round to the nearest $1 before adding to estimate.

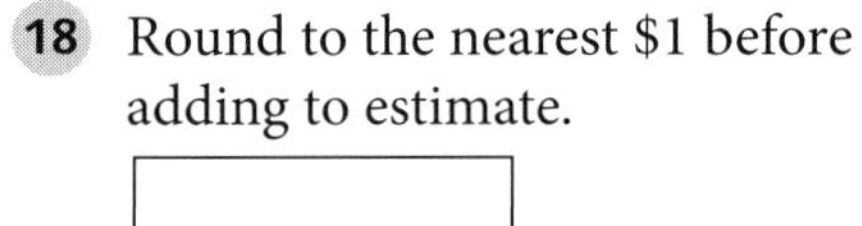

19 Find the difference between 10.05 and 4.63.

20 Colour the largest number.

14.361 14.631 14.639 14.360

21 Round each number to the nearest hundred.

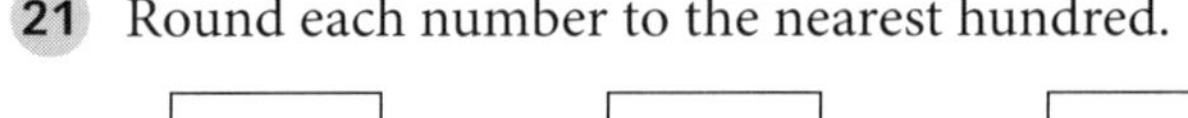

9985 ☐ 18 637 ☐ 24 278 ☐

22 Complete the number pattern.

10, 50, 250, ☐, ☐, ☐

1 Find the total of 114 836, 92 817 and 43 108.

2 What is the difference between the values on the two cards?

80 396 | 107 947

3 What is 63 groups of 4285?

4

$$90\,000 \div 4 =$$

5

$$\frac{3}{10} + \frac{1}{2} =$$

6 Complete the number line.

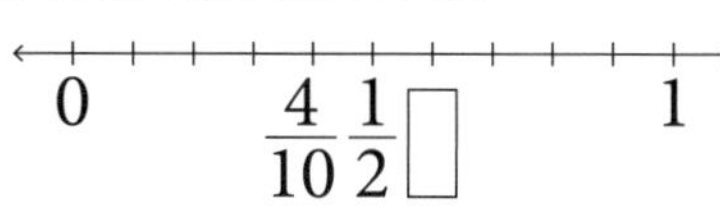

7

$$4 + (7 \times 6) - 30 =$$

8 Draw 9:10 on the clock.

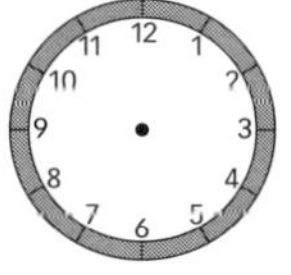

9 Convert 20:50 to am/pm time.

10

$$8.3 \text{ cm} + 40 \text{ mm} =$$

11 Find the perimeter.

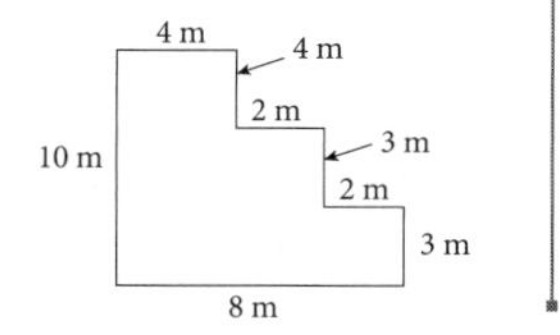

12 Circle the greatest volume.

11 000 mL   10 L

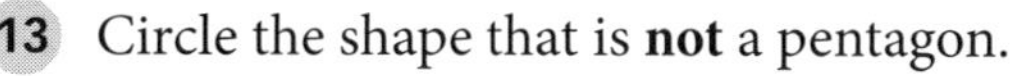

13 Circle the shape that is **not** a pentagon.

  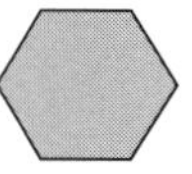 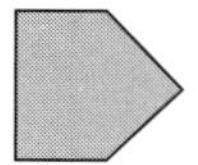

14 Name this 3D shape.

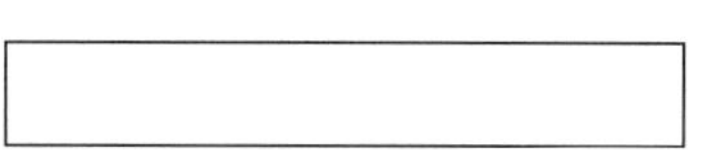

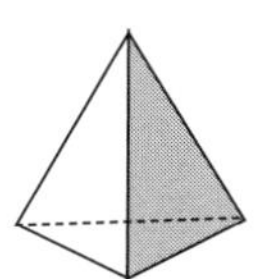

15 Reflect the shape about the mirror line.

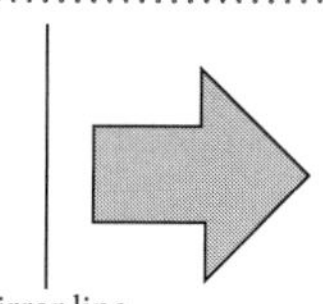

16 Draw a triangle at (0, 3).

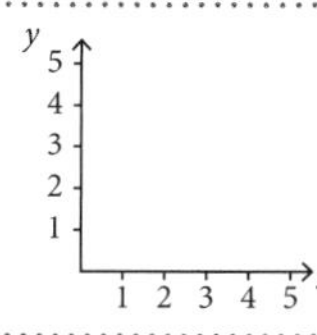

17 Estimate the size of this angle.

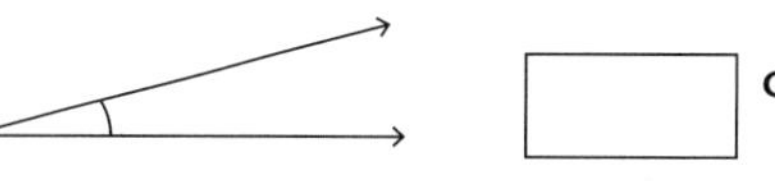

°

18 What is the chance (as a fraction) that a circle will be selected?

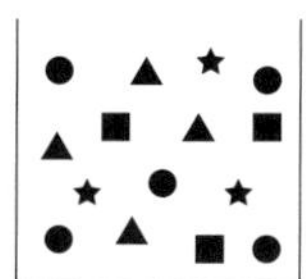

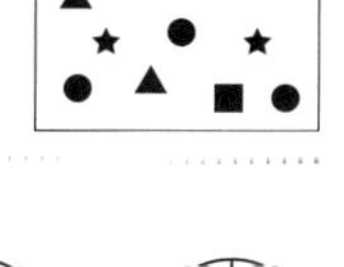

19 Circle the spinner that has a $\frac{3}{4}$ chance of white being selected.

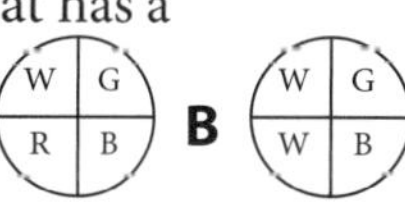

20 How many more basketballs than volleyballs did the school have?

Ball	Number
football	56
basketball	47
netball	29
soccer ball	72
volleyball	19

21 How many sheep and goats are at the farm altogether?

22 Add 25 alpacas to the graph.

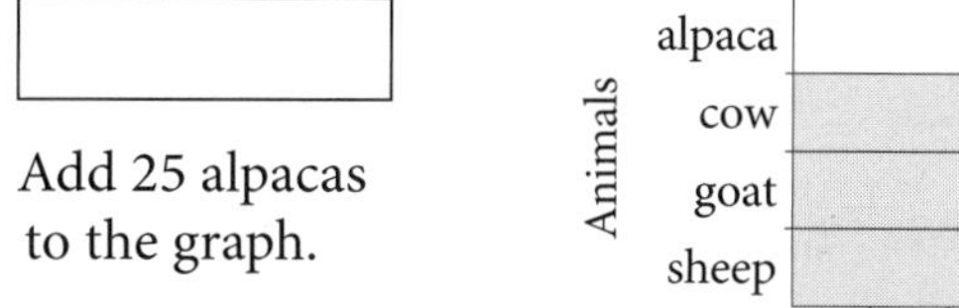

1

+	29	14	18	23	31	9
23						

2

–	48	21	46	32	41	50
19						

3

×	3	9	11	7	4	1
6						

4

×	2	6	10	8	12	5
7						

5

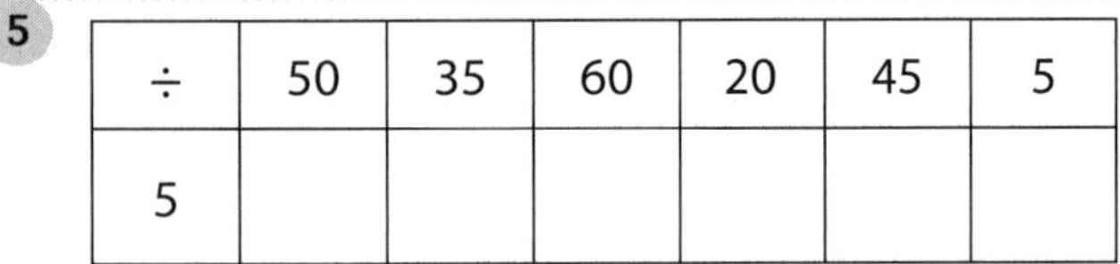

÷	50	35	60	20	45	5
5						

6

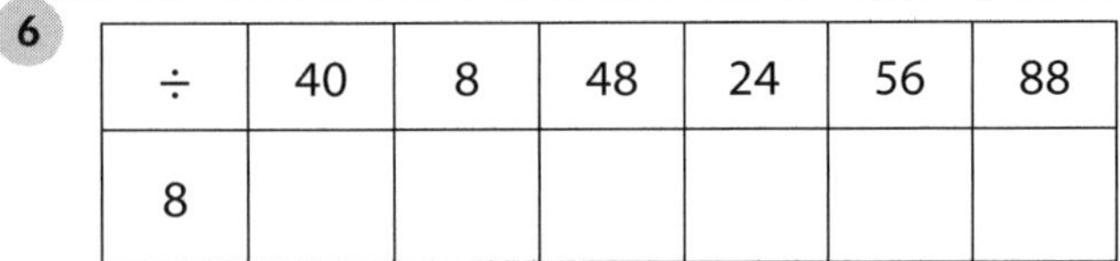

÷	40	8	48	24	56	88
8						

7

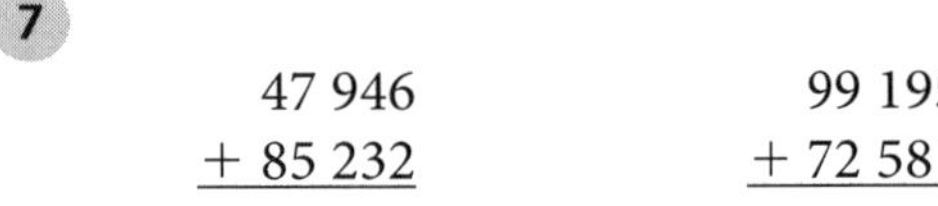

$$\begin{array}{r} 47\,946 \\ +\ 85\,232 \\ \hline \end{array} \qquad \begin{array}{r} 99\,195 \\ +\ 72\,581 \\ \hline \end{array}$$

8 Find the sum of 900 000 and 40 000.

9 How much more is needed to make 19 000 from 8505?

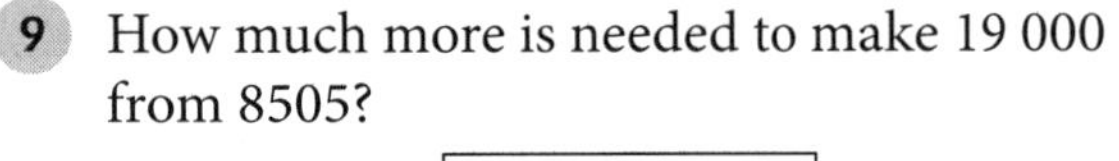

10 Use the number line to show 143 – 87 = ☐

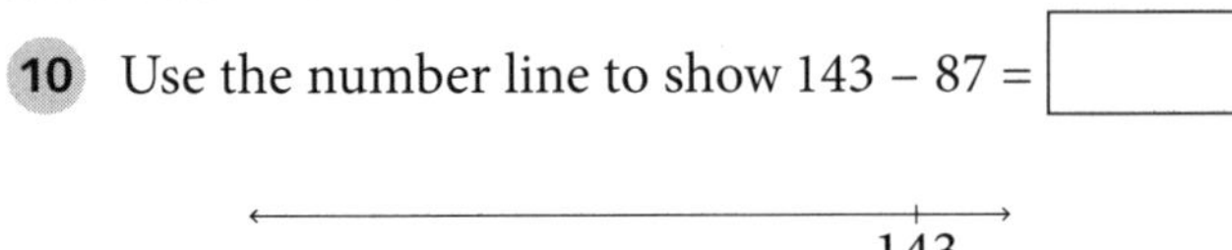

11

$$\begin{array}{r} 50 \\ \times\ \ 7 \\ \hline \end{array} \qquad \begin{array}{r} 90 \\ \times\ \ 4 \\ \hline \end{array}$$

12 Find the total cost of 40 movie tickets at $9 each.

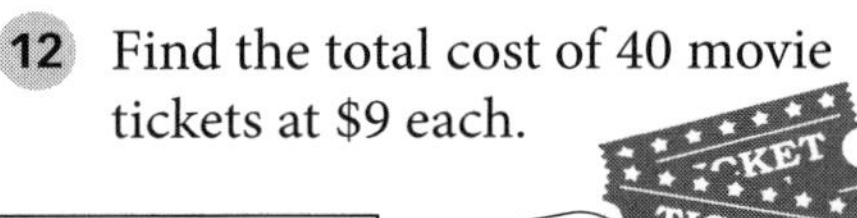

13

$$60 \div 7 = \square$$

14

$$8\overline{)824}$$

15 True or false? 15 is a prime number.

16 Order the numbers from smallest to largest.

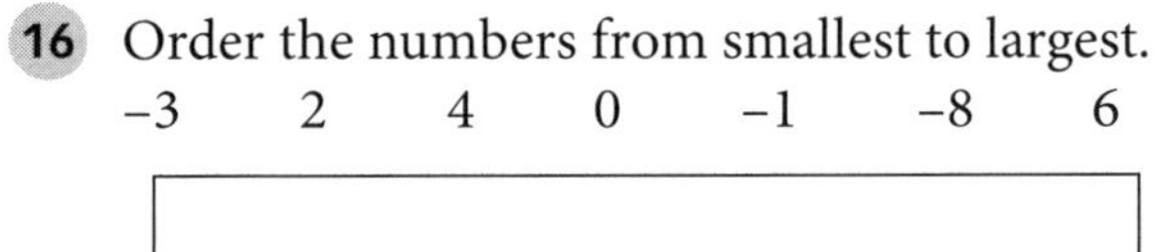

–3 2 4 0 –1 –8 6

17 Find the change from $900.

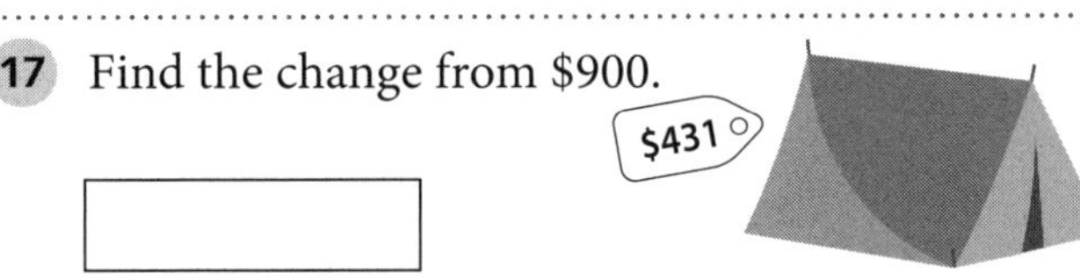

18 Round to the nearest $1 before adding to estimate.

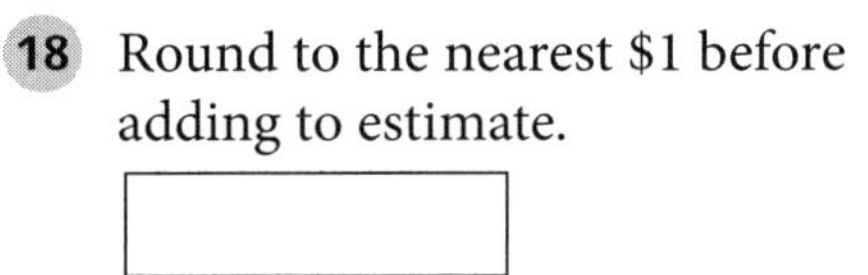

19 Find the difference between 20.46 and 17.96.

20 Colour the largest number.

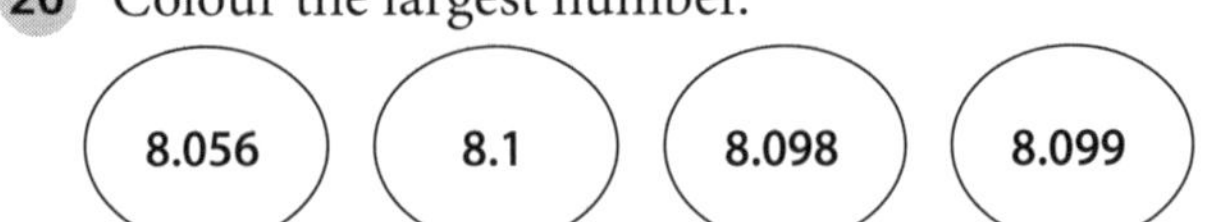

21 Round each number to the nearest hundred.

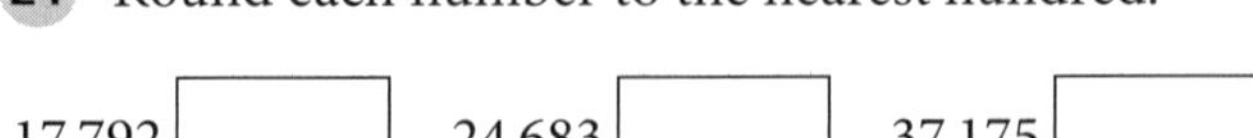

17 792 ☐ 24 683 ☐ 37 175 ☐

22 Complete the number pattern.

1, 10, 100, ☐, ☐, ☐

1 Find the total of 48 963, 52 108 and 110 479.

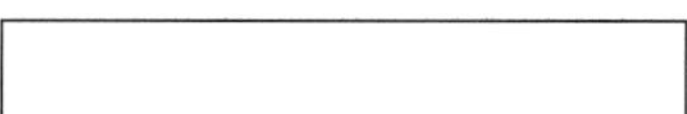

2 What is the difference between the values on the two cards?

110 847	32 168	

3 What is 27 groups of 5679?

4

$50\,000 \div 3 =$ ☐

5

$\frac{1}{5} + \frac{3}{10} =$ ☐

6 Complete the number line.

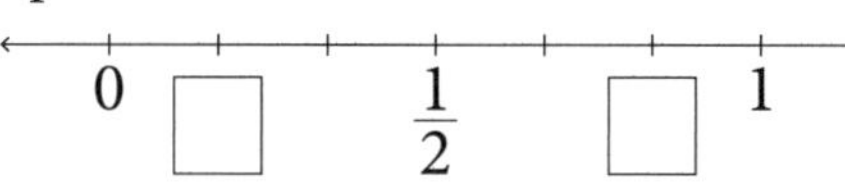

7

$2 \times (7 + 9) - 20 =$ ☐

8 Draw 2:40 on the clock.

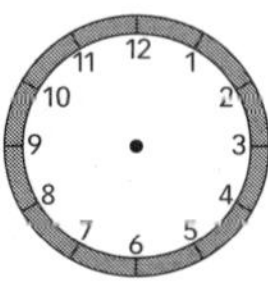

9 Convert 19:05 to am/pm time.

10

7.1 cm + 0.6 m = ☐

11 Find the perimeter.

4 m
5 m
6 m
5 m
4 m

12 Circle the greatest volume.

13 Circle the shape that is **not** a square.

14 Name this 3D shape.

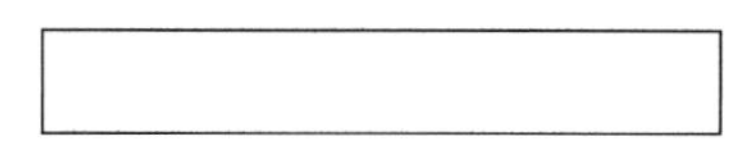

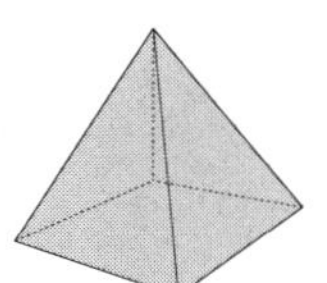

15 Reflect the shape about the mirror line.

16 Draw a dot at (0, 4).

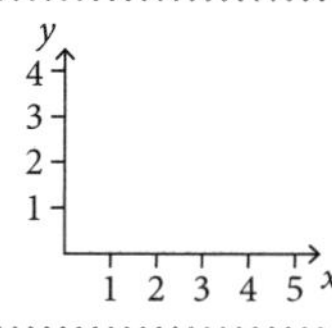

17 Estimate the size of this angle.

☐ °

18 What is the chance (as a fraction) that the letter A will be selected?

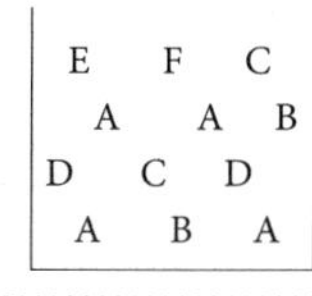

19 Circle the spinner that has a $\frac{3}{8}$ chance of white being selected.

A
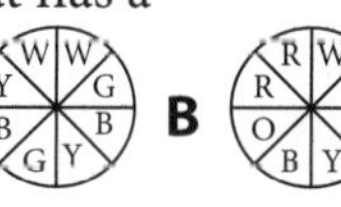

B C
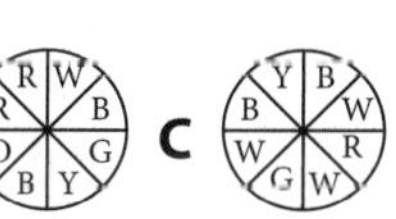

20 How many more cars than vans were in the car park?

Vehicle	Number
truck	11
car	127
motorbike	29
van	37
ute	56

21 How many picture books and comic books are in the library altogether?

22 Add 39 mystery books to the graph.

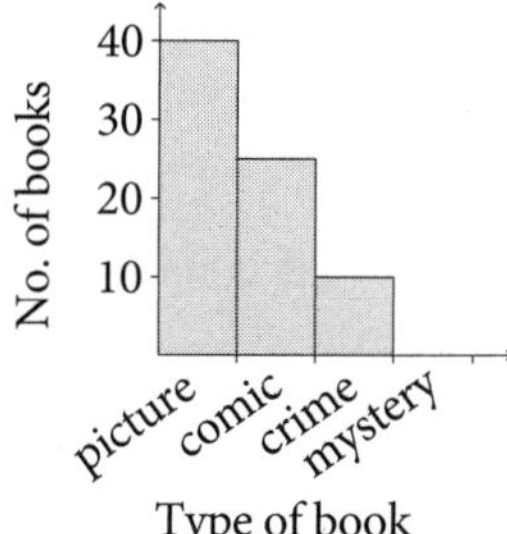

UNIT **11A**

1

+	18	41	25	29	6	35
49						

2

–	56	88	96	72	46	100
38						

3

×	4	7	3	8	9	1
9						

4

×	2	10	5	11	6	12
3						

5

÷	24	6	16	2	8	20
2						

6

÷	77	56	21	42	14	70
7						

7

18 000 + 27 000 = ☐

8 There are 1526 sheets of paper in one pile and 1425 in another pile. What is the total number of sheets of paper? ☐

9

$$\begin{array}{r} 49\,603 \\ -\ 12\,747 \\ \hline \end{array}$$

10

627 831 kg minus 471 200 kg = ☐ kg

11 What is 9 times 6?

☐

12

60 × 60 = ☐

50 × 70= ☐

13

$7\overline{)196}$ $7\overline{)296}$

14

91 shared into 6 groups = ☐

15 Place –7 on the number line.

–10 0 10

16 Circle the composite numbers.

2 5 8 9 11

17 What is 50% of $10?

☐

18 Add $43.29, $87.49 and $211.99.

☐

19 Jack has 9.1 L of water in one bucket and 3.6 L of water in another bucket.
How much water does Jack have altogether? ☐

9.1 L 3.6 L

20

20 – 6.93 = ☐

21 Round each number to the nearest 1000.

14 798 ☐ 23 667 ☐ 84 105 ☐

22 Complete the number pattern.

1.5, 3, 4.5, ☐, ☐, ☐

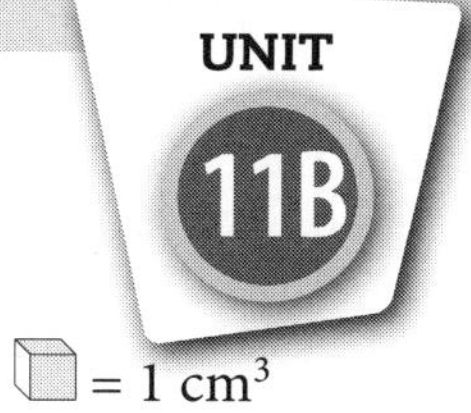

1 What is the total height of the three tallest mountains in the world?

Everest	8848 m
K2	8611 m
Kangchenjunga	8586 m

2

$876\,392 - 531\,798 =$ ☐

3

$60\,000 \times 3 =$ ☐

$60\,000 \times 30 =$ ☐

$60\,000 \times 300 =$ ☐

4

$1\,200\,404 \div 4 =$ ☐

5 What is $\frac{1}{3}$ of 60?

6 Complete:

$1 - \frac{1}{4} =$ ☐

7

$4 \times 9 =$ ☐

$36 \div 4 =$ ☐

$36 \div 9 =$ ☐

8 How many seconds are in 3 minutes? ☐

How many minutes are in 2 hours? ☐

9 What is the difference between the two times?

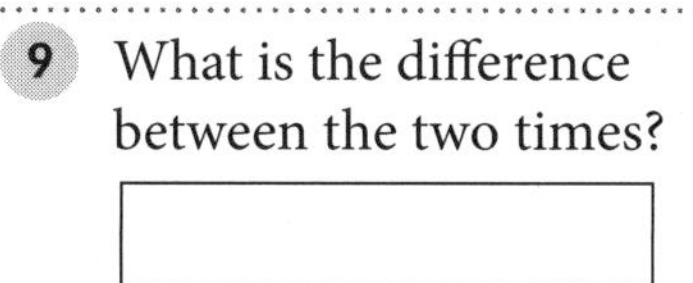

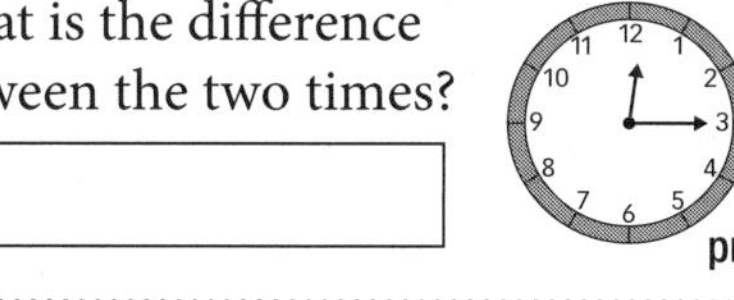

10 Find 600 g + 1.2 kg.

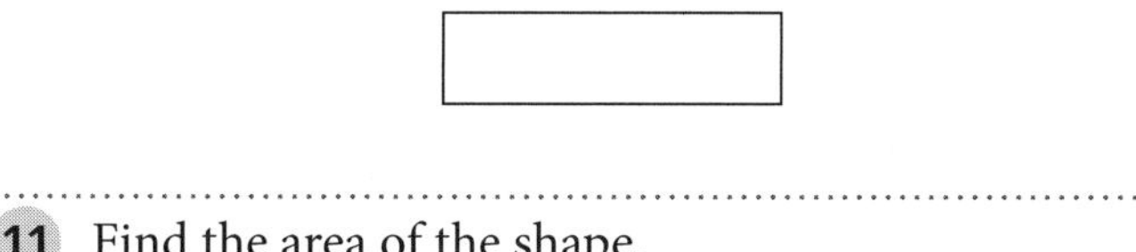

11 Find the area of the shape.

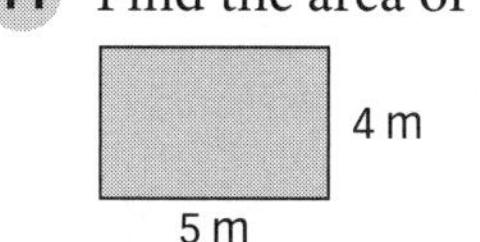

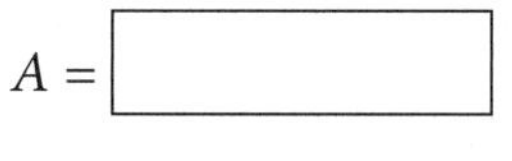

12 Find the volume of:

☐ cm^3

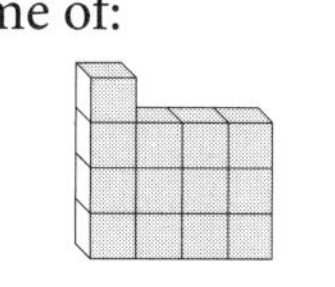

☐ = 1 cm^3

13 Which shapes make up this composite shape?

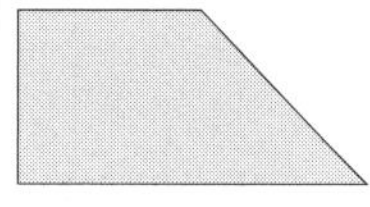

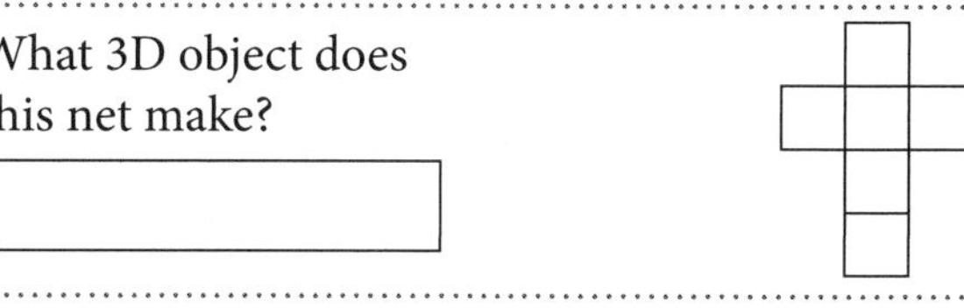

14 What 3D object does this net make?

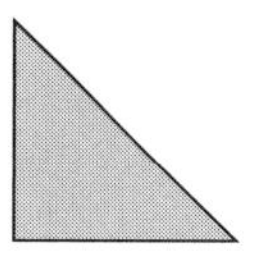

15 Rotate the triangle one quarter turn clockwise.

16 Give the coordinates for the points *A* and *B*.

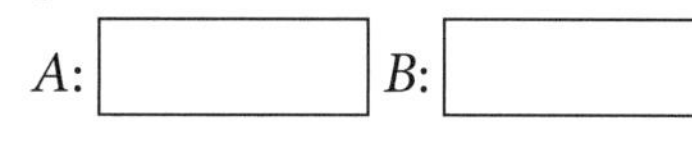

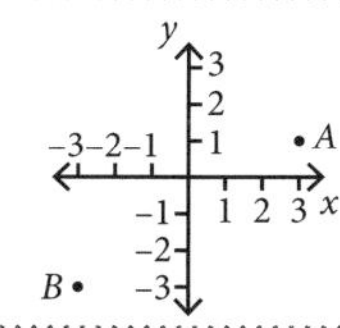

17 Measure the size of the angle.

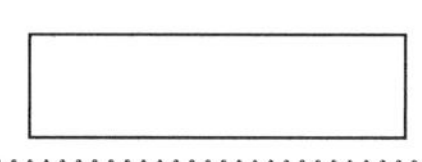

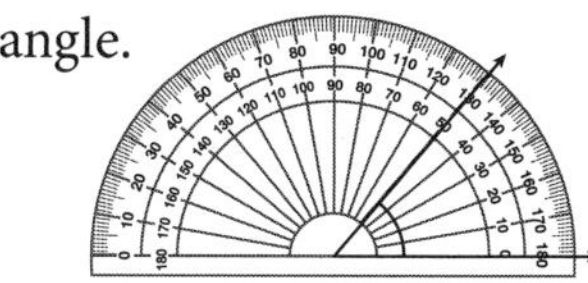

18 What is the chance of getting an odd number when rolling a standard 6-sided dice?

19 The chance of selecting a letter is:

A 0.2 **B** 0.3 **C** 0.5

Which has the greatest chance of occurring?

20 How many students like green and red?

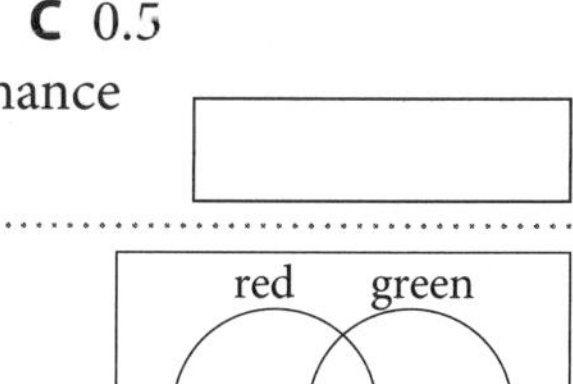

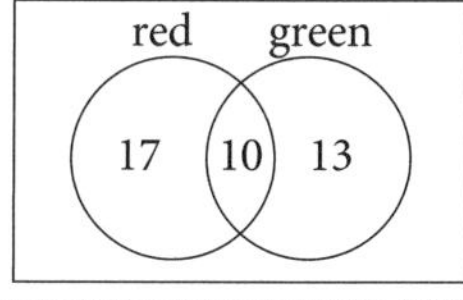

21 What was the height of the plant on the third day?

22 Between which two days did the plant grow the most?

UNIT 12A

1

+	37	18	29	40	12	53
41						

2

–	90	72	86	61	53	29
26						

3

×	4	10	12	3	6	7
9						

4

×	1	5	8	11	2	9
3						

5

÷	4	18	12	10	24	6
2						

6

÷	77	35	28	14	42	84
7						

7

37 000 + 46 000 = ☐

8 There are 2631 sheep in one paddock and 1472 sheep in another paddock. How many sheep are there altogether? ☐

9

$$\begin{array}{r} 72\,463 \\ -\ 19\,347 \\ \hline \end{array}$$

10

372 800 m minus 280 900 m = ☐

11 What does 7 groups of 8 equal?

☐

12

90 × 70 = ☐

50 × 80 = ☐

13

$6\overline{)428}$ $6\overline{)173}$

14

85 shared into 8 groups = ☐

15 Place –3 on the number line.

–10 0 10

16 Circle the composite numbers.

3 4 12 17 21

17 What is 50% of $8?

☐

18 Add $26.28, $97.35 and $115.87.

☐

19 There is 6.83 kg of potatoes on the scales and Jill adds another 3.25 kg of potatoes. What is the total weight of the potatoes? ☐

6.83 kg 3.25 kg

20

17 – 12.63 = ☐

21 Round each number to the nearest 1000.

330 691 ☐ 242 783 ☐ 181 005 ☐

22 Complete the number pattern.

1, 1.7, 2.4, ☐, ☐, ☐

1 What is the total depth of three of the deepest oceanic trenches in the world?

Mariana Trench	11 033 m
Tonga Trench	10 882 m
Kuril-Kamchatka Trench	10 500 m

2 $708\,321 - 468\,598 =$ ______

3 $90\,000 \times 4 =$ ______

$90\,000 \times 40 =$ ______

$90\,000 \times 400 =$ ______

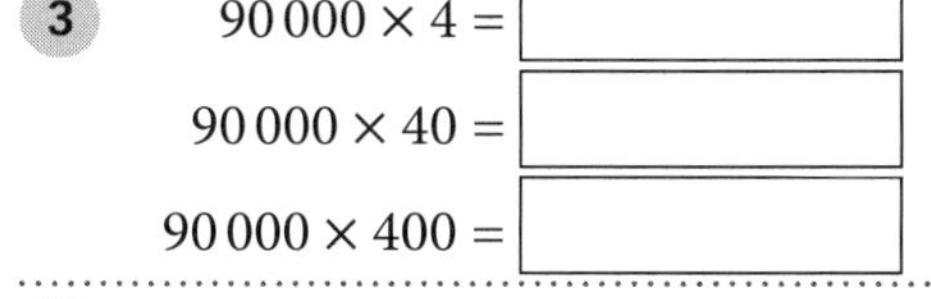

4 $1\,306\,900 \div 3 =$ ______

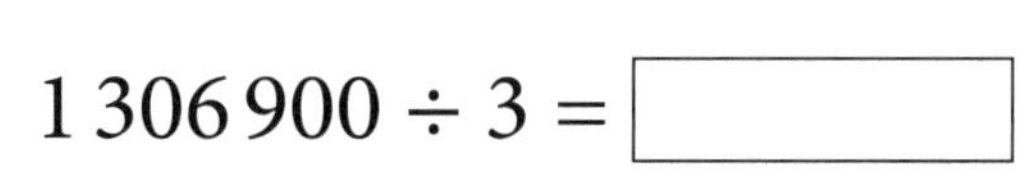

5 What is $\frac{1}{5}$ of 30?

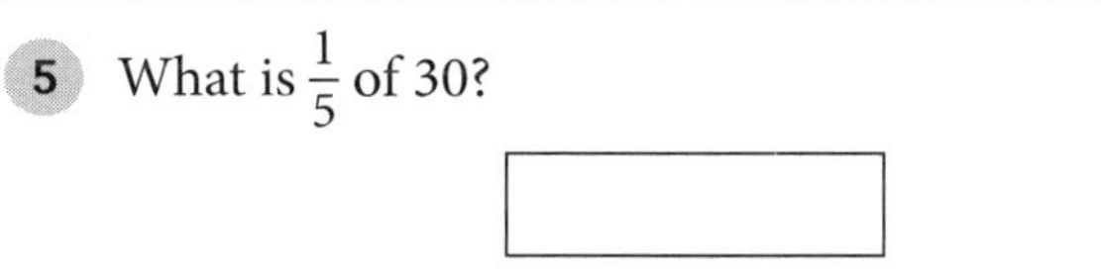

6 Complete:

$1 - \frac{2}{5} =$ ______

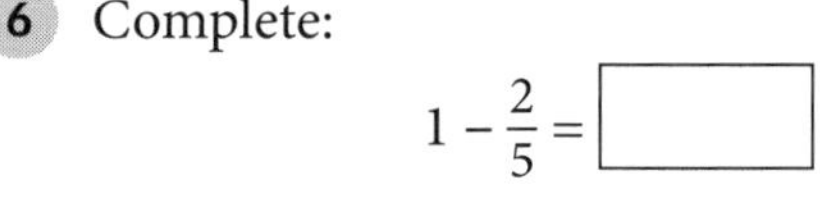

7 $7 \times 12 =$ ______

$84 \div 7 =$ ______

$84 \div 12 =$ ______

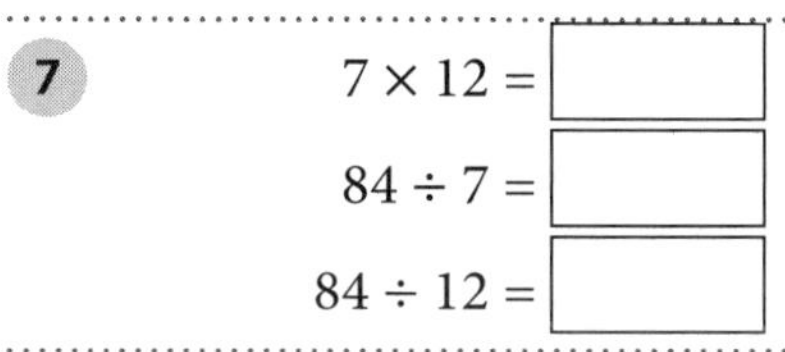

8 How many seconds are in 2 minutes? ______

How many minutes are in 4 hours? ______

9 What is the difference between the two times?

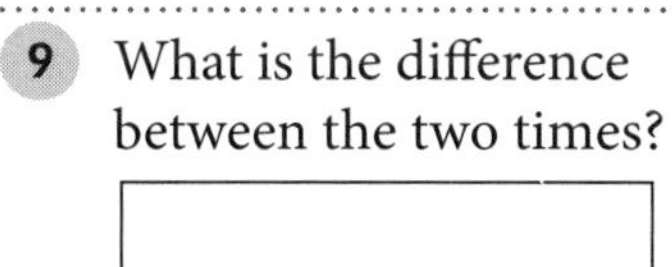

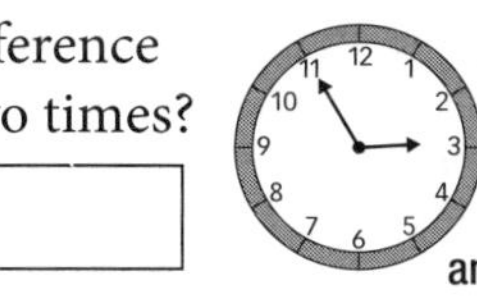

10 Find 900 g + 1.3 kg.

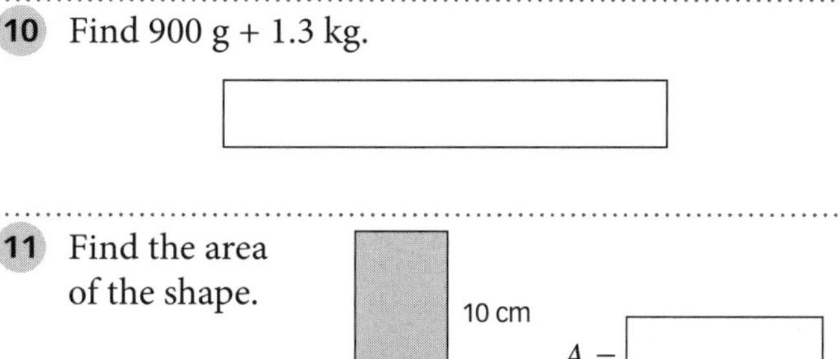

11 Find the area of the shape.

10 cm

2 cm

$A =$ ______

12 What is the volume of the shape?

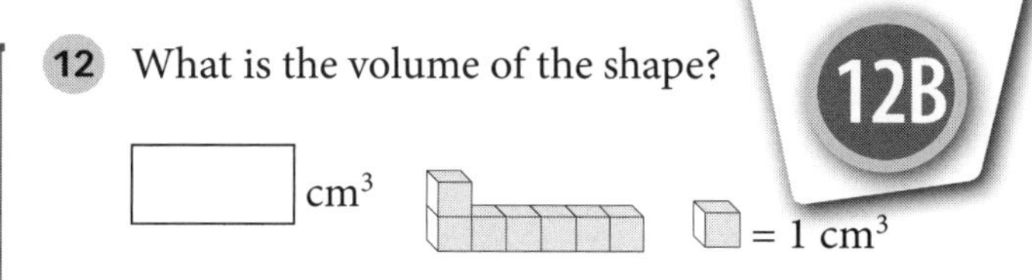

______ cm^3 = 1 cm^3

13 Which shapes make up this composite shape?

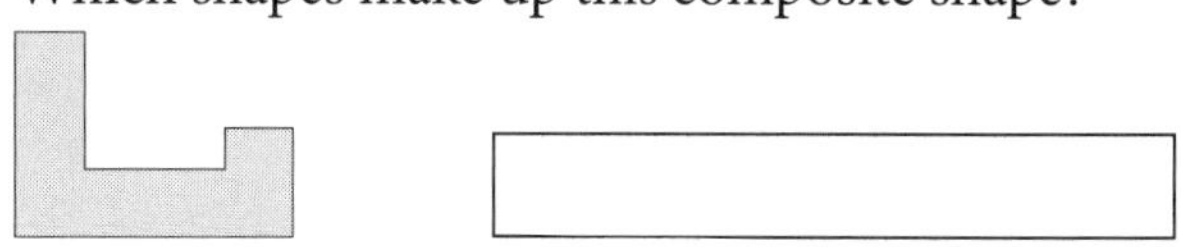

14 What 3D object does this net make?

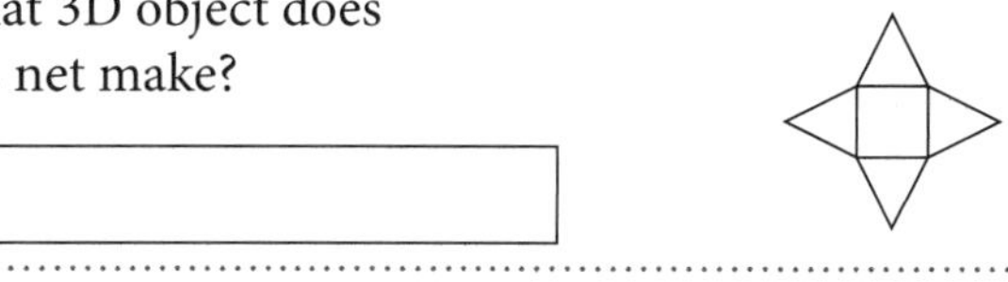

15 Rotate the triangle one half turn clockwise.

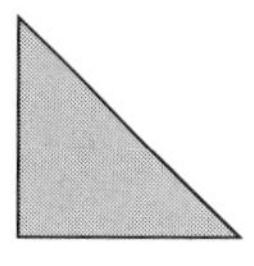

16 Give the coordinates for the points A and B.

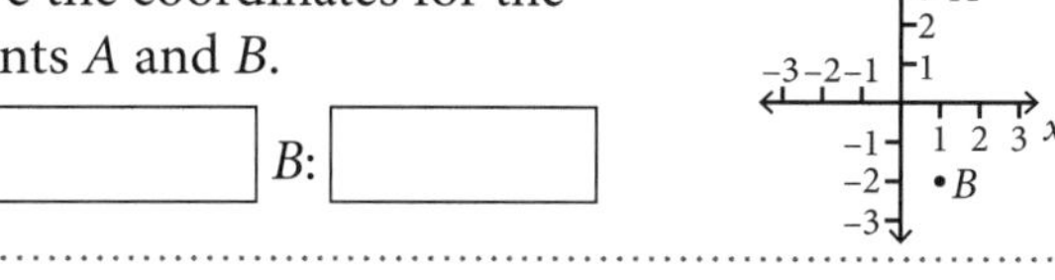

A: ______ B: ______

17 Measure the size of the angle.

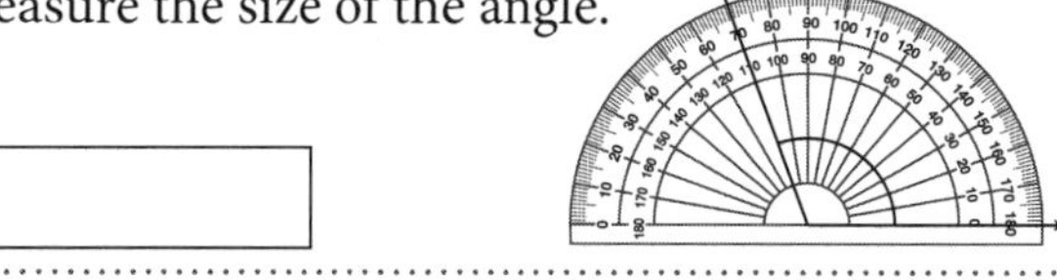

18 What is the chance of getting an even number when rolling a standard 6-sided dice?

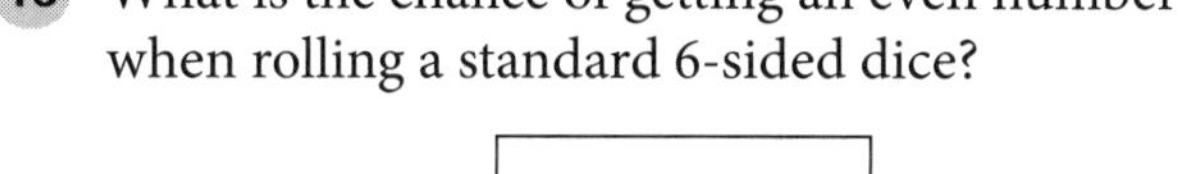

19 The chance of selecting a letter is:

A 0.1 **B** 0.2 **C** 0.7

Which is the least chance of occurring?

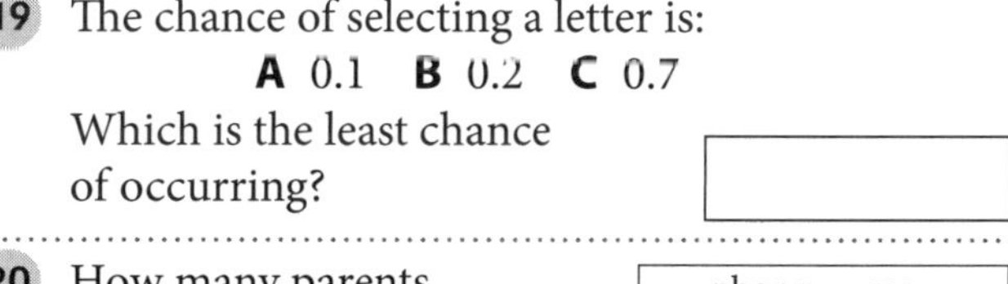

20 How many parents have a car and a phone?

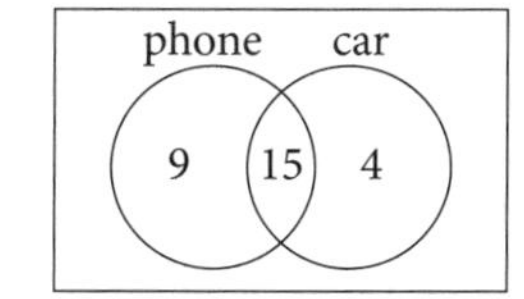

21 How much profit did the coffee shop make in March?

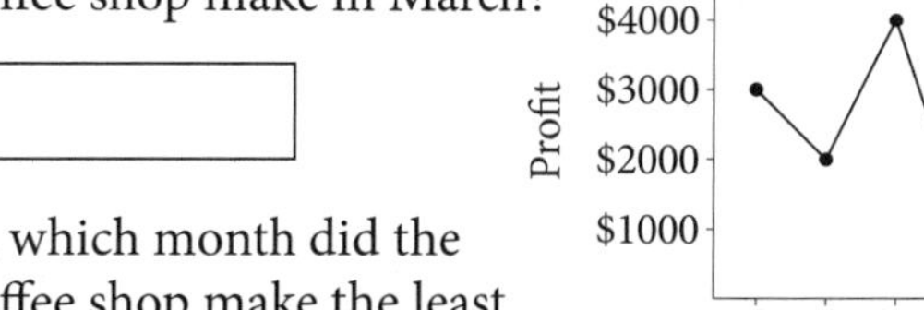

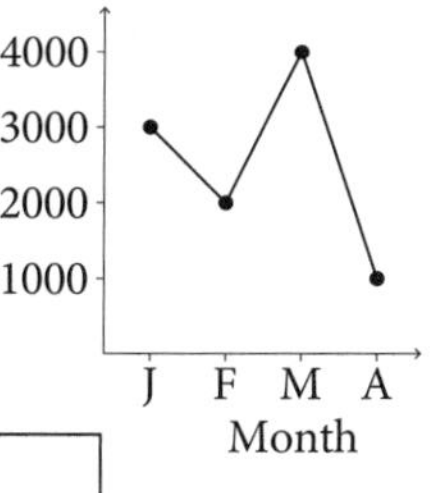

22 In which month did the coffee shop make the least amount of profit?

1

+	42	26	46	20	38	19
38						

2

–	70	40	92	33	51	89
32						

3

×	4	12	8	10	1	6
9						

4

×	2	5	9	3	11	7
3						

5

÷	2	22	6	12	8	16
2						

6

÷	7	84	49	14	28	70
7						

7

58 000 + 27 000 = ☐

8 There are 1320 bananas in one warehouse and 2426 bananas in another warehouse. How many bananas are there altogether? ☐

9

  63 127
− 47 649

10

261 489 mm minus 196 400 mm = ☐

11 What is 12 multiplied by 6? ☐

12

80 × 90 = ☐

30 × 20 = ☐

13

$5\overline{)179}$ $5\overline{)246}$

14

90 shared into 7 groups = ☐

15 Place –1 on the number line.

–10   0   10

16 Circle the composite numbers.

6 10 17 23 35

17 What is 50% of $22? ☐

18 Add $89.45, $117.87 and $221.23. ☐

19 Sue measures a piece of wood to be 3.95 m long. She measures a second piece to be 4.85 m long. What is the total length of the wood? ☐

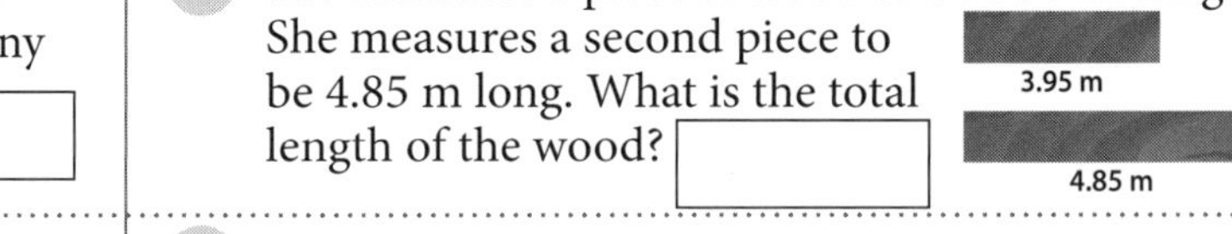

20

12 – 11.07 = ☐

21 Round each number to the nearest 1000.

142 785 ☐ 196 117 ☐ 135 483 ☐

22 Complete the number pattern.

9, 9.3, 9.6, ☐, ☐, ☐

UNIT 13B

1 What is the total height of the three tallest buildings in the world? [ ]

Burj Khalifa	828 m
Shanghai Tower	632 m
Makkah Royal Clock Tower	601 m

2 $846\,308 - 294\,763 =$ [ ]

3 $40\,000 \times 6 =$ [ ]

$40\,000 \times 60 =$ [ ]

$40\,000 \times 600 =$ [ ]

4 $1\,408\,906 \div 8 =$ [ ]

5 What is $\frac{1}{3}$ of 36? [ ]

6 Complete:

$1 - \frac{3}{10} =$ [ ]

7 $8 \times 7 =$ [ ]

$56 \div 7 =$ [ ]

$56 \div 8 =$ [ ]

8 How many seconds are in 5 minutes? [ ]

How many minutes are in 5 hours? [ ]

9 What is the difference between the two times? [ ]

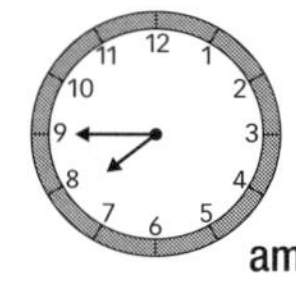

10 Find 800 g + 1.4 kg. [ ]

11 Find the area of the shape.

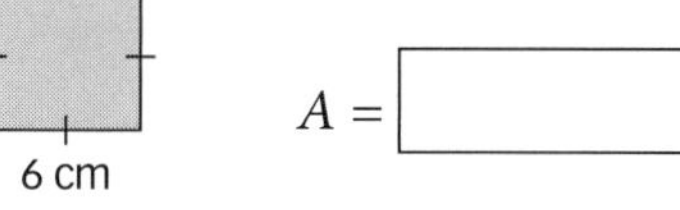

$A =$ [ ]

12 What is the volume of the shape?

[ ] cm^3

= 1 cm^3

13 Which shapes make up this composite shape?

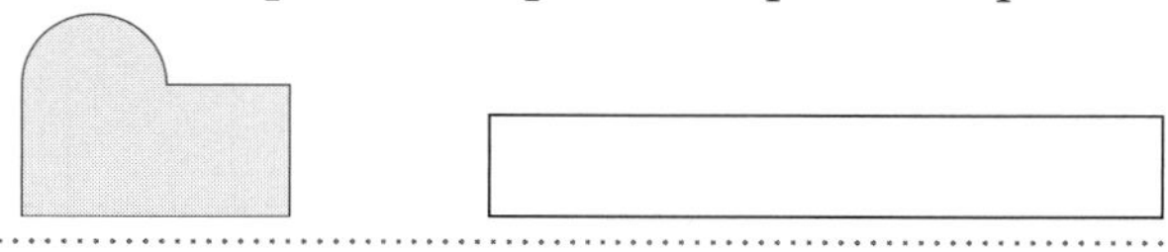

[ ]

14 What 3D object does this net make? [ ]

15 Rotate the rectangle one quarter turn anticlockwise.

16 Give the coordinates for the points A and B.

A: [ ] B: [ ]

17 Measure the size of the angle. [ ]

18 What is the chance of getting a number less than 5 when rolling a standard 6-sided dice? [ ]

19 The chance of selecting a letter is:

A 0.7 **B** 0.1 **C** 0.2

Which is the greatest chance of occurring? [ ]

20 How many people only liked broccoli? [ ]

cabbage broccoli

6 9 14

21 What was the temperature at 9 am? [ ]

22 What was the difference in temperature between 11 am and 12 noon? [ ]

Temperature (°C)

Time

8 am 9 am 10 am 11 am 12 pm

UNIT 14A

1

+	17	39	43	26	52	8
47						

2

–	90	51	28	77	32	46
19						

3

×	4	6	11	7	9	1
9						

4

×	2	10	8	3	12	5
3						

5

÷	20	12	2	10	18	6
2						

6

÷	14	35	70	63	49	21
7						

7

71 000 + 39 000 = ☐

8 There are 1495 hats in one delivery and 1347 hats in another delivery. How many hats are there altogether? ☐

9

$$\begin{array}{r} 83\,746 \\ -\ 56\,329 \\ \hline \end{array}$$

10

120 300 L minus 78 920 L = ☐

11 What does 6 lots of 10 equal? ☐

12

80 × 70 = ☐

30 × 80= ☐

13

$7\overline{)193}$ $7\overline{)478}$

14

76 shared into 4 groups = ☐

15 Place 6 on the number line.

–10 0 10

16 Circle the composite numbers.

7 9 18 19 23 40

17 What is 50% of $36? ☐

18 Add $911.85, $212.48 and $617.99. ☐

19 The height of a beanstalk is 1.52 m and the height of a second beanstalk is 1.17 m. What is the total height of the beanstalks? ☐

1.52 m 1.17 m

20

10 – 3.85 = ☐

21 Round each number to the nearest 1000.

142 785 ☐ 196 117 ☐ 135 483 ☐

22 Complete the number pattern.

18, 18.6, 19.2, ☐, ☐, ☐

1 What is the total length of the three longest rivers in the world?

Amazon River	6992 km
Nile River	6853 km
Yangtze River	6300 km

2 $738\,561 - 472\,846 =$

3 $80\,000 \times 7 =$

$80\,000 \times 70 =$

$80\,000 \times 700 =$

4 $1\,609\,303 \div 6 =$

5 What is $\frac{1}{7}$ of 49?

6 Complete:

$1 - \frac{5}{8} =$

7 $9 \times 6 =$

$54 \div 9 =$

$54 \div 6 =$

8 How many seconds are in 6 minutes?

How many hours are in 2 days?

9 What is the difference between the two times?

10 Find 3 kg + 6000 g.

11 Find the area of the shape.

3 cm

20 cm

$A =$

12 What is the volume of the shape?

cm³

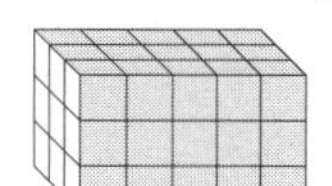

= 1 cm³

13 Which shapes make up this composite shape?

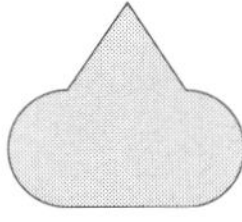

14 What 3D object does this net make?

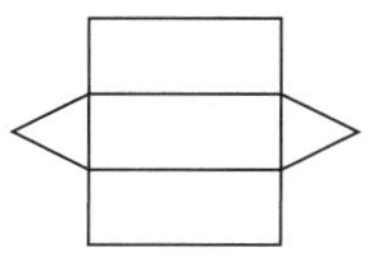

15 Rotate the rectangle one half turn anticlockwise.

16 Give the coordinates for the points A and B.

A: B:

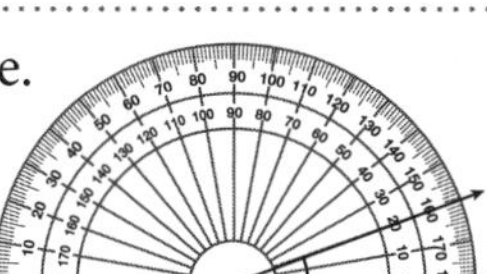

17 Measure the size of the angle.

18 What is the chance of getting a number greater than 5 when rolling a standard 6-sided dice?

19 The chance of selecting a letter is:

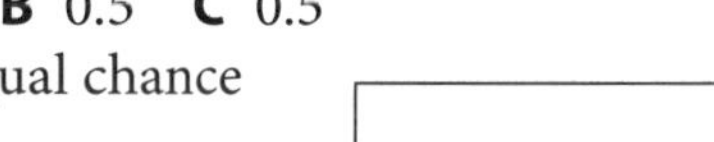

Which have an equal chance of occurring?

20 How many people competed only in swimming?

swimming cycling

15 9 12

21 What was Sara's height when she was 10?

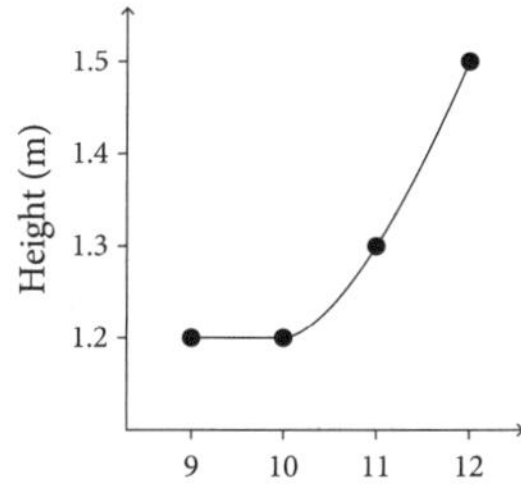

22 When did Sara grow the most?

UNIT 15A

1

+	17	36	9	41	28	55
56						

2

–	100	63	90	79	81	58
45						

3

×	7	5	9	11	12	4
9						

4

×	3	10	1	6	8	2
3						

5

÷	2	10	14	16	22	8
2						

6

÷	84	21	7	49	35	63
7						

7

36 900 + 17 000 = ☐

8 There are 1325 books in one row at the library and 1949 in another row. How many books are there altogether in the two rows? ☐

9

$$\begin{array}{r} 67\,346 \\ -\ 29\,459 \\ \hline \end{array}$$

10

736 845 tonnes minus 149 786 tonnes = ☐

11 What does 9 groups of 11 equal?

☐

12

100 × 90 = ☐

10 × 80 = ☐

13

$4\overline{)437}$ $4\overline{)489}$

14

89 shared into 5 groups = ☐

15 Place –10 on the number line.

–10 0 10

16 Circle the composite numbers.

21 23 17 20 5 40

17 What is 50% of $200?

☐

18 Add $413.39, $317.89 and $515.07.

☐

19 Jan walked 1.69 km on Saturday and 2.58 km on Sunday. How far did Jan walk altogether? ☐

10 SATURDAY 1.69 km

11 SUNDAY 2.58 km

20

16 – 9.34 = ☐

21 Round each number to the nearest 1000.

1 417 803 ☐ 2 792 485 ☐ 8 110 948 ☐

22 Complete the number pattern.

10, 10.06, 10.12, ☐, ☐, ☐

1 What is the total length of three of the longest bridges in the world?

Danyang-Kunshan Grand Bridge	164 800 m
Tianjin Grand Bridge	113 700 m
Weinan Weihe Grand Bridge	79 700 m

2 983 106 − 429 488 =

3 70 000 × 6 =

70 000 × 60 =

70 000 × 600 =

4 1 703 985 ÷ 5 =

5 What is $\frac{1}{4}$ of 48?

6 Complete:

$1 - \frac{2}{3} =$

7 5 × 12 =

60 ÷ 12 =

60 ÷ 5 =

8 How many seconds are in 4 minutes?

How many hours are in 5 days?

9 What is the difference between the two times?

am pm

10 Find 3000 g + 4.5 kg.

11 Find the area of the shape.

9 mm

2 mm

A =

12 What is the volume of the shape?

cm³ = 1 cm³

13 Which shapes make up this composite shape?

14 What 3D object does this net make?

15 Rotate the triangle one three-quarter turn anticlockwise.

16 Give the coordinates for the points *A* and *B*.

A: *B*:

17 Measure the size of the angle.

18 What is the chance of getting the numbers 2, 3 or 4 when rolling a standard 6-sided dice?

19 The chance of selecting a number is:

A 0 **B** 0.7 **C** 0.3

Which is the greatest chance of occurring?

20 How many students have both white and black socks?

white black

10 9 11

21 How high was the tide at 4 pm?

22 What was the highest the tide reached?

Height (m): 0.6, 0.8, 1, 1.2, 1.4

Time: 3 pm, 4 pm, 5 pm, 6 pm, 7 pm

1

+	31	14	28	17	21	40
29						

2

−	80	67	36	43	20	72
18						

3

×	6	2	10	7	12	4
6						

4

×	1	8	5	9	11	3
7						

5

÷	25	50	45	10	30	60
5						

6

÷	8	32	72	80	40	24
8						

7

$$\begin{array}{r} 79\,387 \\ +\ 12\,463 \\ \hline \end{array}$$

8 What is the sum of 20 000 and 90 000?

9

$$\begin{array}{r} 49\,685 \\ -\ 32\,871 \\ \hline \end{array}$$

10 Use the number line to show 147 – 59 = ☐

147

11 What is 7 multiplied by 12?

12 What is the total cost of 80 towels at $10 each?

$10.00

13

$$7\overline{)196}$$

14 What is 42 shared into 5 groups?

15 True or false? 27 is a prime number.

16 Circle the composite number.

A 9 **B** 13
C 31 **D** 47

17 Find the change from $500 when a phone is bought.

$160

18 What is 50% of 86 kg?

19 Find the difference between 6.32 and 1.79.

20 Which is the largest number?

A 3.78 **B** 3.87
C 3.96 **D** 3.638

21 Round 44 239 to the nearest hundred.

22 Complete the number pattern.

2, 3.5, 5, ☐, ☐

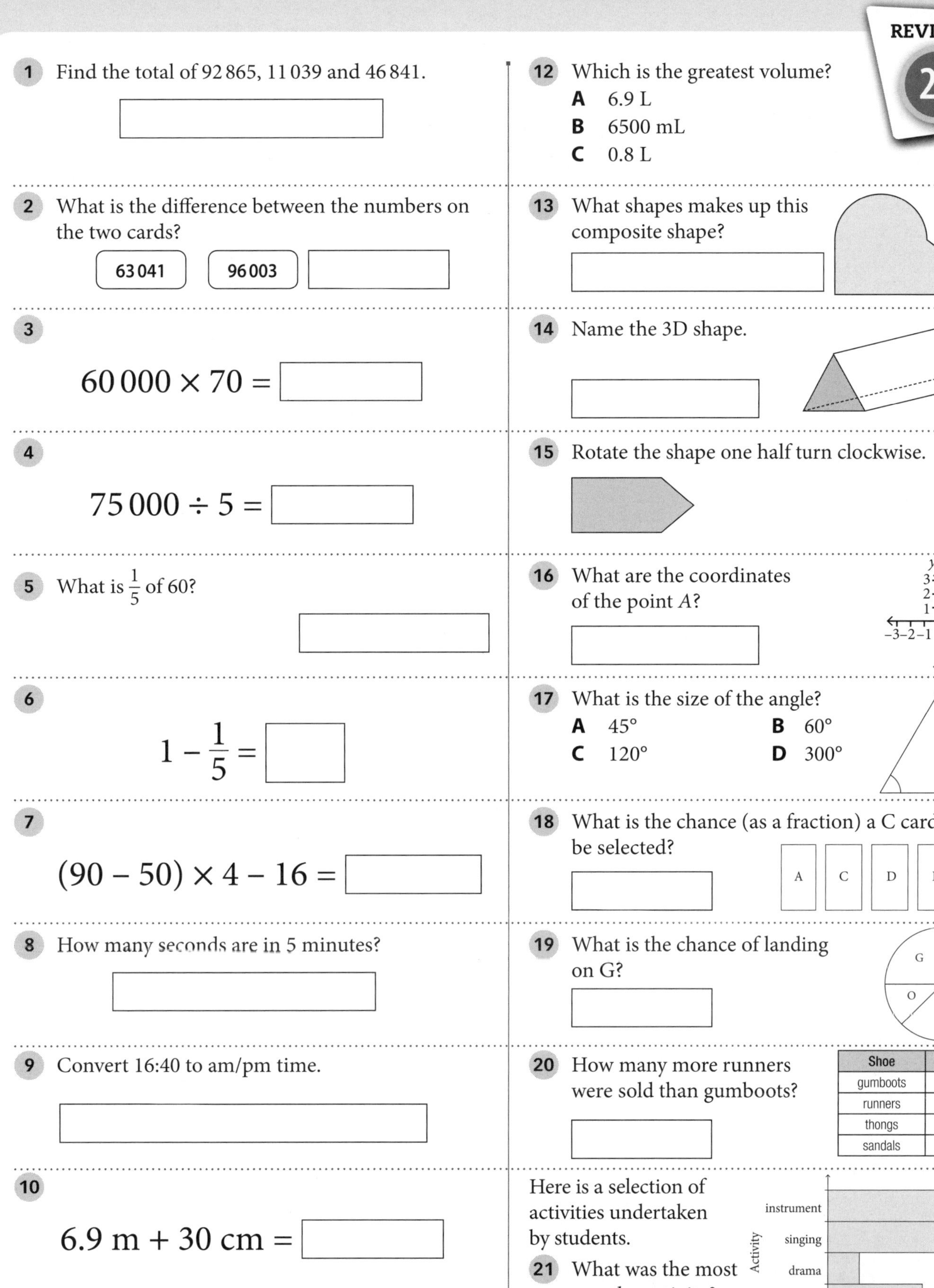

1 Find the total of 92 865, 11 039 and 46 841.

2 What is the difference between the numbers on the two cards?

63 041 | 96 003

3

$60\,000 \times 70 =$

4

$75\,000 \div 5 =$

5 What is $\frac{1}{5}$ of 60?

6

$1 - \frac{1}{5} =$

7

$(90 - 50) \times 4 - 16 =$

8 How many seconds are in 5 minutes?

9 Convert 16:40 to am/pm time.

10

$6.9 \text{ m} + 30 \text{ cm} =$

11 Find the perimeter.

12 Which is the greatest volume?

A 6.9 L

B 6500 mL

C 0.8 L

13 What shapes makes up this composite shape?

14 Name the 3D shape.

15 Rotate the shape one half turn clockwise.

16 What are the coordinates of the point *A*?

17 What is the size of the angle?

A 45° **B** 60°

C 120° **D** 300°

18 What is the chance (as a fraction) a C card will be selected?

19 What is the chance of landing on G?

20 How many more runners were sold than gumboots?

Shoe	Number
gumboots	6
runners	11
thongs	14
sandals	8

Here is a selection of activities undertaken by students.

21 What was the most popular activity?

22 How many more students play instruments than do drama?

1 The number of cars on two levels of a car park were recorded. What was the total number of cars on the two levels?

A 2773
B 2873
C 2883
D 2973

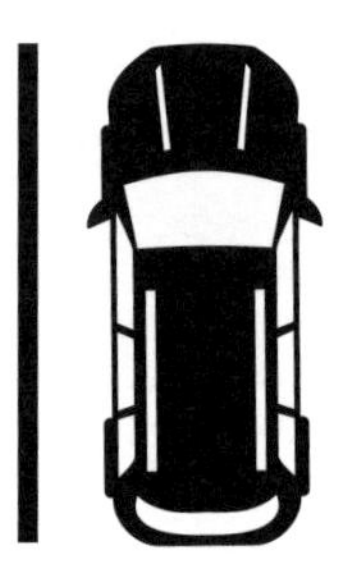

1496
1387

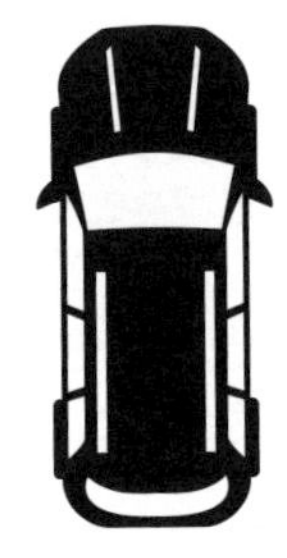

2 Which equation does the number line represent?

A 173 – 50 =
B 173 – 65 =
C 173 – 55 =
D 173 – 60 =

−2 −3 −10 −50

173

3 What is the total cost of 9 T-shirts?

A $84
B $96
C $108
D $120

4 Jack completed the equation. What was Jack's answer?

A 17 r 4
B 18
C 20 r 2
D 21

$$9\overline{)16^{7}2} = 18$$

5 Sally has 4 number cards. Which one is a prime number?

9	11	15	21
A	**B**	**C**	**D**

Answers

Unit 1A page 8

1. 35, 34, 37, 32, 30, 33
2. 27, 12, 8, 23, 21, 5
3. 30, 45, 15, 40, 10, 5
4. 32, 56, 80, 88, 96, 40
5. 5, 6, 3, 7, 2, 12
6. 12, 9, 7, 6, 3, 5
7. 11 000, 16 000
8. 26 810, 25 427
9. 8110
10. 3129
11. 42 days
12. 5400
13. 9, 1
14. 4
15. 42 611
16. 9, 81
17. $12 902
18. $3.50 + $6.50 + $5.00 = $15.00
19. 8.05, 8.33, 8.46, 8.6
20. 21.34
21. 18 410, 29 400, 71 180
22. 17, 23

Unit 1B page 9

1. $2 336 472
2. 718 621
3. 2 520 000
4. 428
5. $\frac{1}{4}$
6. 2, 8
7. 82
8. quarter to 7 or 6:45
9. 4:10 or 10 past 4
10. 125
11. 1.8 m
12. 24
13. rectangle, circle, semicircle
14. 5, 8, 5
15.
16. (3, 2)
17. acute
18. parent/carer to check
19. 1, 2, 3, 4, 5, 6
20. red 12, blue 9, green 7
21. 15
22. 10

Unit 2A page 10

1. 40, 31, 36, 23, 42, 45
2. 35, 20, 28, 4, 16, 31
3. 30, 20, 45, 40, 25, 15
4. 16, 80, 56, 96, 88, 72
5. 12, 8, 9, 6, 2, 11
6. 4, 11, 6, 7, 2, 12
7. 17 000, 13 000
8. 65 245, 33 377
9. 5150
10. 9247
11. 28
12. 1400
13. 8, 8
14. 6
15. 92 790
16. 49, 16
17. $17 968
18. $7 + $8.50 + $7.50 = $23
19. 9.05, 9.2, 9.37, 9.63
20. 11.237
21. 73 890, 24 790, 96 420
22. 40, 48

Unit 2B page 11

1. $1 168 814
2. 882 015
3. 4 480 000
4. 8956
5. $\frac{1}{8}$
6. 2, 9
7. $102
8. quarter past 12 or 12:15
9. 9:00 or 9 o'clock
10. 93
11. 0.4 m
12. 216
13. hexagon, parallelogram, octagon
14. 6, 12, 8
15. 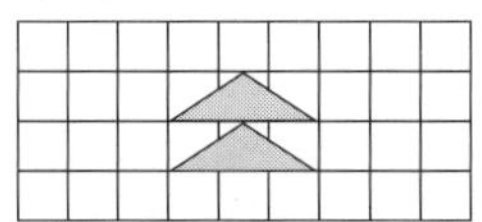
16. (5, 1)
17. reflex
18. parent/carer to check
19. 1, 2, 4, 6
20. small 20, medium 16, large 18
21. 50
22. 190

Unit 3A page 12

1. 46, 38, 29, 33, 44, 55
2. 12, 29, 35, 11, 24, 38
3. 20, 60, 45, 5, 50, 30
4. 16, 56, 88, 24, 64, 40
5. 3, 4, 7, 6, 10, 1
6. 4, 11, 7, 1, 9, 5
7. 11 000, 21 000
8. 114 056, 110 171
9. 9480
10. 4691
11. 49
12. 4800
13. 4, 8
14. 4
15. 116 310
16. 4, 100
17. $7482
18. $9.00 + $6.50 + $7.50 = $23.00
19. 8.143, 8.314, 8.341, 8.431
20. 20.13
21. 41 490, 26 240, 11 110
22. 129, 140

Unit 3B page 13

1. $2 376 736
2. 123 608
3. 3 320 000
4. 892
5. $\frac{1}{8}$
6. 3, 2
7. 750
8. 25 past 7 or 7:25
9. 8:10 or 10 past 8
10. 650
11. 90 cm
12. 28
13. trapezium, square, hexagon
14. 6, 12, 8
15. 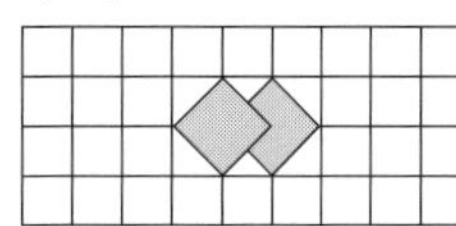
16. (0, 1)
17. straight
18. parent/carer to check
19. 3, 4, 7, 9
20. water 23, juice 13, tea 16, coffee 31
21. 150
22. 4

Unit 4A page 14

1. 39, 42, 28, 21, 32, 48
2. 13, 32, 4, 19, 29, 21
3. 15, 55, 40, 50, 20, 45
4. 16, 48, 0, 96, 56, 40
5. 3, 11, 5, 8, 2, 9
6. 1, 11, 7, 4, 8, 12
7. 15 000, 22 000
8. 109 356, 111 917
9. 42 264
10. 15 240
11. 63
12. 0
13. 6, 12
14. 12
15. 279 503
16. 1, 25
17. $8528
18. $10.50 + $9.50 + $8.00 = $28.00
19. 6.038, 6.083, 6.308, 6.803
20. 23.171
21. 91 010, 26 370, 91 200
22. 132, 182

Unit 4B page 15

1. $1 573 514
2. 615 900
3. 810 000
4. 9887
5. $\frac{1}{9}$
6. 1, 4
7. 11.7 km
8. 1:35 or 25 minutes to 2
9. half past 1 or 1:30
10. 26
11. 19 cm
12. 21
13. pentagon, rectangle, rhombus
14. 5, 9, 6
15. 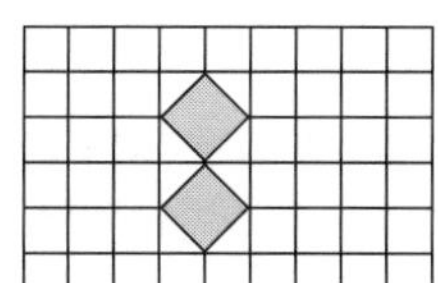
16. (2, 4)
17. acute
18. parent/carer to check
19. 1, 2, 3, 4, 6, 7
20. gold 7, silver 13, bronze 22
21. 75
22. February

Unit 5A page 16

1. 45, 23, 43, 51, 58, 34
2. 2, 33, 4, 19, 7, 30
3. 45, 20, 10, 40, 25, 55
4. 56, 24, 80, 96, 8, 48
5. 2, 8, 9, 6, 10, 1
6. 1, 10, 6, 4, 3, 8
7. 9000, 19 000
8. 76 502, 89 060
9. 36 429
10. 49 230
11. 70
12. 2100
13. 12, 8
14. 10
15. 107 216
16. 36, 64
17. $17 692
18. $7.50 + $9.00 + $4.00 = $20.50
19. 2.134, 2.143, 2.341, 2.431
20. 16.46
21. 17 650, 99 850, 27 120
22. 97, 106

Unit 5B page 17

1. $1 854 276
2. 267 815
3. 25 200 000
4. 7896
5. $\frac{1}{6}$
6. 2, 8
7. 384
8. 11:55 or 5 minutes to 12
9. 3:45 or quarter to 4
10. 450
11. 1.6 m
12. 20
13. triangle, pentagon, parallelogram
14. 4, 6, 4
15. 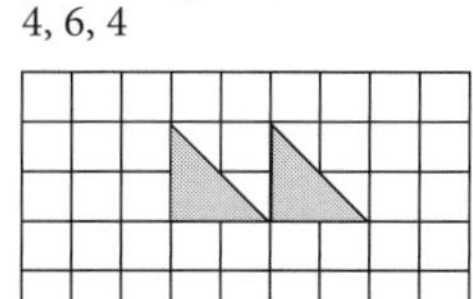
16. (1, 4)
17. reflex
18. parent/carer to check

Answers

19. A, 2, 3, 4, 5, 6, 7, 8, 9, 10, J, Q, K
20. T-shirt 22, shorts 13, jumper 14, hat 3
21. 150
22. 3

Unit 6A page 18

1. 45, 40, 51, 32, 42, 54
2. 7, 22, 10, 18, 27, 31
3. 60, 42, 48, 6, 54, 24
4. 28, 77, 14, 35, 84, 21
5. 2, 5, 10, 3, 9, 1
6. 3, 12, 7, 1, 5, 10
7. 140 855, 43 092
8. 150 000
9. 1790
10. 66
11. 280, 300
12. $800
13. 3 r 2
14. 22
15. true
16. −8, −2, −1, 0, 3, 6
17. $115
18. $14 + $11 + $8 = $33
19. 1.88
20. 3.4
21. 4800, 9400, 1100
22. 27, 81, 243

Unit 6B page 19

1. 149 931
2. 746 257
3. 95 294
4. 7500
5. $\frac{3}{4}$
6. $\frac{3}{10}, \frac{4}{10}$
7. 3
8.

9. 1:00 pm
10. 1.5 m or 150 cm
11. 22 cm
12. 6.1 L
13.
14. rectangular prism
15.
16.
17. 30°
18. $\frac{5}{8}$

19. C
20. 14
21. 500
22. parent/carer to check

Unit 7A page 20

1. 52, 30, 41, 54, 48, 34
2. 25, 17, 3, 33, 9, 22
3. 42, 6, 24, 66, 48, 18
4. 14, 42, 70, 35, 84, 63
5. 6, 3, 12, 9, 1, 11
6. 3, 6, 1, 11, 9, 4
7. 123 376, 81 077
8. 1 100 000
9. 63 995
10. 86
11. 270, 300
12. $60
13. 4 r 2
14. 33
15. true
16. −8, −4, 0, 1, 2, 7
17. $721
18. $18 + $18 + $10 = $46
19. 1.37
20. 7.96
21. 24 000, 72 500, 67 200
22. 16, 32, 64

Unit 7B page 21

1. 219 488
2. 310 538
3. 398 055
4. 7777 r 7
5. $\frac{5}{8}$
6. $\frac{3}{8}, \frac{4}{8} (\frac{1}{2})$
7. 5
8.

9. 11:15 pm
10. 335 mm or 33.5 cm
11. 36 m
12. 9.5 L
13.
14. triangular prism
15.

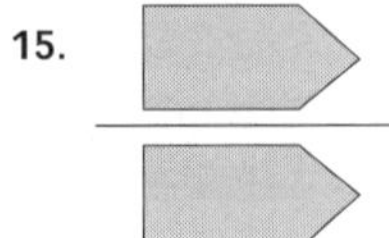

16.
17. 100°
18. $\frac{3}{8}$

19. B
20. 31
21. 200
22. parent/carer to check

Revision 1A page 22

1. 44, 35, 27, 47, 32, 28
2. 27, 8, 5, 24, 13, 20
3. 5, 30, 20, 35, 50, 60
4. 64, 16, 72, 88, 24, 40
5. 12, 9, 5, 3, 7, 1
6. 9, 4, 2, 8, 5, 3
7. 17 000
8. A
9. 14 240
10. 93 182
11. C
12. 990
13. 5 r 5
14. 8
15. D
16. 81
17. $1170
18. $6.00 + $4.00 + $4.50 = $14.50
19. 1.53
20. 12.234, yes
21. 65 000
22. 32, 40, 48

Revision 1B page 23

1. $106 100
2. $630 589
3. 600 000
4. 1000
5. $\frac{4}{8} = \frac{1}{2}$
6. $\frac{1}{2} (\frac{2}{4})$
7. 3
8.

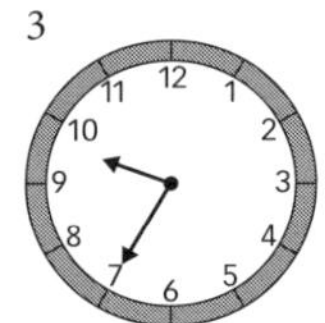

9. 3:55
10. 49
11. B
12. 240
13. C
14. 6
15. C

mirror line

16. (2, 3)
17. D
18. $\frac{4}{8} = \frac{1}{2}$
19. 1, 3, 4, 7
20. 12
21. 200
22. 50

NAPLAN-style Test 1 pages 24–27

1. D
2. A
3. C
4. B
5. D
6. A
7. C
8. A
9. 36
10. A
11. $\frac{1}{4}$
12. C
13. C
14. 270
15. B
16. D
17. D
18. C
19. 2, 4, 6, 8, 10, 12
20. 500

Unit 8A page 28

1. 32, 37, 43, 52, 46, 34
2. 29, 8, 25, 32, 4, 14
3. 54, 48, 42, 24, 6, 18
4. 14, 70, 42, 77, 35, 84
5. 12, 1, 8, 6, 3, 11
6. 5, 4, 2, 3, 7, 9
7. 67 057, 117 263
8. 1 100 000
9. 8291
10. 68
11. 140, 360
12. $630
13. 6 r 4
14. 21
15. false
16. −9, −8, 1, 3, 6, 7
17. $650
18. $4 + $8 + $12 = $24
19. 2.87
20. 4.7
21. 67 800, 21 100, 39 400
22. 64, 256, 1024

Unit 8B page 29

1. 493 240
2. 17 902
3. 531 432
4. 16 000
5. $\frac{5}{6}$
6. $\frac{2}{4} (\frac{1}{2}), \frac{3}{4}$
7. 434
8.

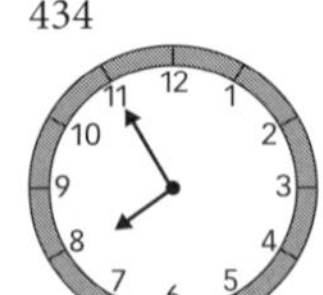

9. 3:30 pm
10. 10.2 m or 1020 cm
11. 22 cm
12. 6500 mL
13.

14. rectangular prism
15.

Answers

16.

17. 160°
18. $\frac{3}{10}$
19. C
20. 56
21. 25
22. parent/carer to check

Unit 9A page 30

1. 40, 27, 48, 38, 44, 59
2. 22, 10, 33, 2, 29, 13
3. 24, 18, 54, 60, 72, 6
4. 14, 42, 56, 35, 77, 49
5. 10, 5, 3, 9, 6, 12
6. 1, 2, 12, 3, 10, 6
7. 116 884, 86 524
8. 170 000
9. 12 092
10. 72
11. 280, 240
12. $150
13. 6 r 2
14. 102
15. true
16. −4, −2, 0, 1, 2, 6, 8
17. $611
18. $17 + $22 + $5 = $44
19. 5.42
20. 14.639
21. 10 000, 18 600, 24 300
22. 1250, 6250, 31 250

Unit 9B page 31

1. 250 761
2. 27 551
3. 269 955
4. 22 500
5. $\frac{8}{10} = \frac{4}{5}$
6. $\frac{6}{10}$
7. 16
8. 
9. 8:50 pm
10. 12.3 cm or 123 mm
11. 36 m
12. 11 000 mL
13. 
14. triangular-based pyramid
15.

16. 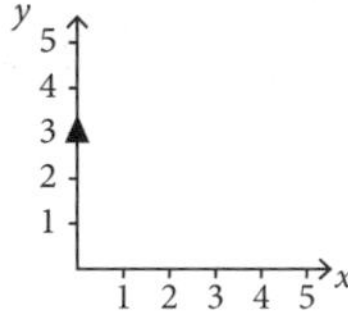

17. 15°
18. $\frac{5}{15} = \frac{1}{3}$
19. C
20. 28
21. 650
22. parent/carer to check

Unit 10A page 32

1. 52, 37, 41, 46, 54, 32
2. 29, 2, 27, 13, 22, 31
3. 18, 54, 66, 42, 24, 6
4. 14, 42, 70, 56, 84, 35
5. 10, 7, 12, 4, 9, 1
6. 5, 1, 6, 3, 7, 11
7. 133 178, 171 776
8. 940 000
9. 10 495
10. 56
11. 350, 360
12. $360
13. 8 r 4
14. 103
15. false
16. −8, −3, −1, 0, 2, 4, 6
17. $469
18. $22 + $10 + $6 = $38
19. 2.5
20. 8.1
21. 17 800, 24 700, 37 200
22. 1000, 10 000, 100 000

Unit 10B page 33

1. 211 550
2. 78 679
3. 153 333
4. 16 666 r 2
5. $\frac{5}{10}$ ($\frac{1}{2}$)
6. $\frac{1}{6}$, $\frac{5}{6}$
7. 12
8. 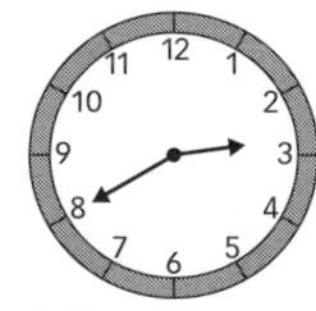
9. 7:05 pm
10. 67.1 cm or 0.671 m
11. 24 m
12. 9.2 L
13.
14. square-based pyramid
15. 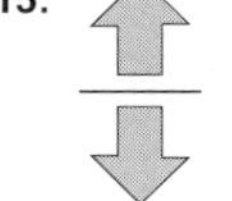

16.

17. 170°
18. $\frac{4}{12} = \frac{1}{3}$
19. C
20. 90
21. 65
22. parent/carer to check

Unit 11A page 34

1. 67, 90, 74, 78, 55, 84
2. 18, 50, 58, 34, 8, 62
3. 36, 63, 27, 72, 81, 9
4. 6, 30, 15, 33, 18, 36
5. 12, 3, 8, 1, 4, 10
6. 11, 8, 3, 6, 2, 10
7. 45 000
8. 2951
9. 36 856
10. 156 631
11. 54
12. 3600, 3500
13. 28, $42\frac{2}{7}$
14. 15 r 1
15. parent/carer to check
16. 8, 9
17. $5
18. $342.77
19. 12.7 L
20. 13.07
21. 15 000, 24 000, 84 000
22. 6, 7.5, 9

Unit 11B page 35

1. 26 045 m
2. 344 594
3. 180 000, 1 800 000, 18 000 000
4. 300 101
5. 20
6. $\frac{3}{4}$
7. 36, 9, 4
8. 180 seconds, 120 minutes
9. 2 hours 40 minutes
10. 1.8 kg or 1800 g
11. 20 m^2
12. 13
13. square, triangle
14. cube
15. 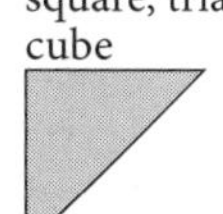
16. A (3, 1) B (−3, −3)
17. 50°
18. $\frac{1}{2}$ ($\frac{3}{6}$)
19. C
20. 10
21. 4 cm
22. from day 3 to day 4 (grew from 4 cm on 3rd day to 7 cm on 4th day)

Unit 12A page 36

1. 78, 59, 70, 81, 53, 94
2. 64, 46, 60, 35, 27, 3
3. 36, 90, 108, 27, 54, 63
4. 3, 15, 24, 33, 6, 27
5. 2, 9, 6, 5, 12, 3
6. 11, 5, 4, 2, 6, 12
7. 83 000
8. 4103
9. 53 116
10. 91 900 m
11. 56
12. 6300, 4000
13. $71\frac{1}{3}$, $28\frac{5}{6}$
14. 10 r 5
15. parent/carer to check
16. 4, 12, 21
17. $4
18. $239.50
19. 10.08 kg
20. 4.37
21. 331 000, 243 000, 181 000
22. 3.1, 3.8, 4.5

Unit 12B page 37

1. 32 415 m
2. 239 723
3. 360 000, 3 600 000, 36 000 000
4. 435 633 r1
5. 6
6. $\frac{3}{5}$
7. 84, 12, 7
8. 120 seconds, 240 minutes
9. 4 hours 50 minutes
10. 2.2 kg or 2200 g
11. 20 cm^2
12. 7
13. rectangles
14. square-based pyramid
15. 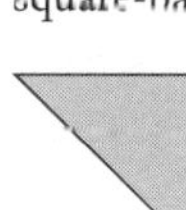
16. *A* (1, 3), *B* (1, −2)
17. 110°
18. $\frac{1}{2}$ ($\frac{3}{6}$)
19. A
20. 15
21. $4000
22. April

Unit 13A page 38

1. 80, 64, 84, 58, 76, 57
2. 38, 8, 60, 1, 19, 57
3. 36, 108, 72, 90, 9, 54
4. 6, 15, 27, 9, 33, 21
5. 1, 11, 3, 6, 4, 8

Answers

6. 1, 12, 7, 2, 4, 10
7. 85 000
8. 3746
9. 15 478
10. 65 089 mm
11. 72
12. 7200, 600
13. $35\frac{4}{5}$, $49\frac{1}{5}$
14. 12 r 6
15. parent/carer to check
16. 6, 10, 35
17. $11
18. $428.55
19. 8.8 m
20. 0.93
21. 143 000, 196 000, 135 000
22. 9.9, 10.2, 10.5

Unit 13B page 39

1. 2061 m
2. 551 545
3. 240 000, 2 400 000, 24 000 000
4. 176 113 r2
5. 12
6. $\frac{7}{10}$
7. 56, 8, 7
8. 300 seconds, 300 minutes
9. 2 hours 20 minutes
10. 2.2 kg or 2200 g
11. 36 cm^2
12. 7
13. semicircle, rectangle
14. rectangular prism
15.
16. *A* (–3, 2), *B* (2, –1)
17. 140°
18. $\frac{4}{6}$ or $\frac{2}{3}$
19. A
20. 14
21. 5 °C
22. 5 °C

Unit 14A page 40

1. 64, 86, 90, 73, 99, 55
2. 71, 32, 9, 58, 13, 27
3. 36, 54, 99, 63, 81, 9
4. 6, 30, 24, 9, 36, 15
5. 10, 6, 1, 5, 9, 3
6. 2, 5, 10, 9, 7, 3
7. 110 000
8. 2842
9. 27 417
10. 41 380 L
11. 60
12. 5600, 2400
13. $27\frac{4}{7}$, $68\frac{2}{7}$
14. 19
15. parent/carer to check
16. 9, 18, 40
17. $18
18. $1742.32
19. 2.69 m
20. 6.15
21. 143 000, 196 000, 135 000
22. 19.8, 20.4, 21

Unit 14B page 41

1. 20 145 km
2. 265 715
3. 560 000, 5 600 000, 56 000 000
4. 268 217 r1
5. 7
6. $\frac{3}{8}$
7. 54, 6, 9
8. 360 seconds, 48 hours
9. 4 hours 5 minutes
10. 9 kg or 9000 g
11. 60 cm^2
12. 45
13. triangle, semicircle, square
14. triangular prism
15. 
16. *A* (2, 0), *B* (–3, 0)
17. 20°
18. $\frac{1}{6}$
19. B and C
20. 15
21. 1.2 m
22. between the ages of 11 and 12

Unit 15A page 42

1. 73, 92, 65, 97, 84, 111
2. 55, 18, 45, 34, 36, 13
3. 63, 45, 81, 99, 108, 36
4. 9, 30, 3, 18, 24, 6
5. 1, 5, 7, 8, 11, 4
6. 12, 3, 1, 7, 5, 9
7. 53 900
8. 3274
9. 37 887
10. 587 059 tonnes
11. 99
12. 9000, 800
13. $109\frac{1}{4}$, $122\frac{1}{4}$
14. 17 r 4
15. parent/carer to check
16. 21, 20, 40
17. $100
18. $1246.35
19. 4.27 km
20. 6.66
21. 1 418 000, 2 792 000, 8 111 000
22. 10.18, 10.24, 10.30

Unit 15B page 43

1. 358 200 m
2. 553 618
3. 420 000, 4 200 000, 42 000 000
4. 340 797
5. 12
6. $\frac{1}{3}$
7. 60, 5, 12
8. 240 seconds, 120 hours
9. 2 hours 40 minutes
10. 7.5 kg or 7500 g
11. 18 mm^2
12. 40
13. trapezium and rectangle OR triangle and rectangle
14. triangular-based pyramid
15. 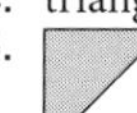
16. *A* (0, 2), *B* (3, 0)
17. 160°
18. $\frac{3}{6}$ ($\frac{1}{2}$)
19. B
20. 9
21. 1.2 m
22. 1.4 m

Revision 2A page 44

1. 60, 43, 57, 46, 50, 69
2. 62, 49, 18, 25, 2, 54
3. 36, 12, 60, 42, 72, 24
4. 7, 56, 35, 63, 77, 21
5. 5, 10, 9, 2, 6, 12
6. 1, 4, 9, 10, 5, 3
7. 91 850
8. 110 000
9. 16 814
10. 88
11. 84
12. $800
13. 28
14. 8 r 2
15. false
16. A
17. $340
18. 43 kg
19. 4.53
20. C
21. 44 200
22. 6.5, 8

Revision 2B page 45

1. 150 745
2. 32 962
3. 4 200 000
4. 15 000
5. 12
6. $\frac{4}{5}$
7. 144
8. 300 seconds
9. 4:40 pm
10. 7.2 m or 720 cm
11. 24 m
12. A
13. triangle, rectangle, semicircle or semicircle and trapezium
14. triangular prism
15. 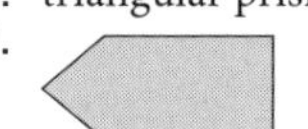
16. (3, 0)
17. B
18. $\frac{2}{5}$
19. $\frac{1}{4}$ or 25%
20. 5
21. singing
22. 30

NAPLAN-style Test 2 pages 46–49

1. C
2. B
3. C
4. B
5. B
6. B
7. $24
8. A
9. A
10. A
11. C
12. 180
13. C
14. 21 m
15. B
16.
17. C
18. B
19. motorbike
20. C

Unit 16A page 50

1. 67, 81, 56, 72, 30, 48
2. 87, 61, 36, 54, 40, 73
3. 12, 40, 20, 48, 32, 8
4. 60, 110, 10, 90, 70, 40
5. 10, 4, 1, 5, 3, 12
6. 9, 4, 8, 2, 6, 1
7. 3900 + 2300 = 6200
8. 878 m
9. 554 825 kg
10. $3450
11. 420, 4200
12. 8, 24
13. 60, 40
14. $2\frac{2}{5}$ pieces each
15. 109 000
16. 3 °C
17. $23.45, $48.50, $66.40
18. 30c
19. 14.56 m
20. 62.97
21. 13 850, 49 600, 77 400
22. add 0.3

Answers

Unit 16B page 51

1. 441 317
2. 20 998.4 g
3. 240 000, 480 000, 540 000
4. true
5. $\frac{7}{6} = 1\frac{1}{6}$
6. 4
7. 4
8. 19:55
9. 5:20 pm
10. 9.5
11. B (A = 10 cm, B = 12 cm)
12. $<$
13. 3, 6, 9, 12
14. circle
15. 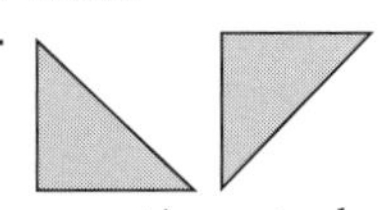
16. parent/carer to check
17. 60°
18. 10%
19. 50% or $\frac{1}{2}$ or 0.5
20. 7
21. $\frac{1}{4}$
22. truck

Unit 17A page 52

1. 71, 56, 40, 69, 83, 47
2. 76, 51, 33, 24, 40, 65
3. 4, 48, 20, 28, 40, 12
4. 60, 110, 20, 90, 80, 40
5. 1, 7, 2, 11, 9, 6
6. 1, 4, 6, 7, 10, 12
7. 5000 + 9300 = 14 300
8. 1914 cm
9. 727 583 m
10. $3670
11. 400, 4000
12. 18, 3
13. 50, 40
14. $2\frac{4}{7}$ pieces of cake each
15. 670 000
16. −4 °C
17. $33.45, $118.00, $213.80
18. 90c
19. 9.78 m
20. 84.26
21. 24 750, 78 500, 69 400
22. add 0.11

Unit 17B page 53

1. 1 257 898
2. 296.75 cm
3. 210 000, 350 000, 490 000
4. true
5. $\frac{17}{12} = 1\frac{5}{12}$
6. 18
7. 52
8. 22:10
9. 6:00 pm
10. 6000
11. Both have the same perimeter of 14 cm.
12. $>$
13. 4, 8, 12, 16
14.
15. 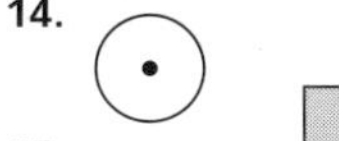
16. parent/carer to check
17. 10°
18. 70%
19. 50%
20. 15
21. $\frac{1}{4}$
22. $\frac{1}{8}$

Unit 18A page 54

1. 61, 82, 59, 68, 76, 47
2. 16, 22, 66, 51, 30, 9
3. 16, 36, 8, 32, 40, 20
4. 60, 110, 10, 70, 120, 30
5. 1, 10, 8, 9, 12, 6
6. 2, 10, 5, 11, 8, 3
7. 61 400 + 7500 = 68 900
8. 2351 mm
9. 102 176 L
10. $3830
11. 180, 1800
12. 4, 20
13. 120, 80
14. $3\frac{4}{7}$ oranges each
15. 176 000
16. 0 °C
17. $74.30, $819.65, $117.55
18. 80c
19. 10.8 L
20. 754.38
21. 61 150, 71 400, 92 200
22. add 0.04

Unit 18B page 55

1. 1 366 610
2. 137 000 kg
3. 450 000, 350 000, 200 000
4. false
5. $\frac{7}{10}$
6. 15
7. 48 + 48 = 96
8. 20:05
9. 4:45 pm
10. 7.5 L
11. Both have the same perimeter of 22 cm.
12. $<$
13. 4, 8, 12, 16
14. square
15.
16. parent/carer to check
17. 45°
18. 90%
19. $\frac{1}{4}$ or 25% or 0.25
20. 20
21. red and green
22. $\frac{1}{4}$

Unit 19A page 56

1. 57, 90, 77, 101, 85, 69
2. 41, 23, 10, 39, 58, 60
3. 8, 48, 24, 28, 36, 16
4. 100, 50, 30, 110, 10, 80
5. 9, 5, 11, 4, 6, 12
6. 11, 5, 9, 12, 7, 3
7. 72 400 + 29 500 = 101 900
8. 2540 km
9. 630 041 m
10. $2810
11. 320, 3200
12. 10, 60
13. 50, 70
14. $4\frac{2}{7}$ bars each
15. 201 000
16. 7 °C
17. $412.95, $612.60, $98.20
18. $1.10
19. 22.47 m
20. 187.75
21. 41 850, 91 900, 61 600
22. subtract 0.03

Unit 19B page 57

1. 1 372 897
2. 1781 cm
3. 320 000, 480 000, 640 000
4. false
5. $\frac{13}{12} = 1\frac{1}{12}$
6. 24
7. 102
8. 03:25
9. 8:30 pm
10. 9.4 L
11. A (A has a perimeter of 24 m and B has a perimeter of 14 m.)
12. $<$
13. 6, 12, 18, 24
14. 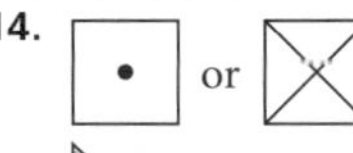
15.
16. parent/carer to check
17. 65°
18. 50%
19. 25%
20. 22
21. $\frac{1}{4}$
22. $\frac{1}{2}$

Unit 20A page 58

1. 71, 95, 68, 109, 112, 86
2. 46, 21, 6, 32, 15, 50
3. 20, 16, 36, 4, 44, 28
4. 20, 100, 80, 120, 60, 30
5. 1, 5, 12, 3, 11, 6
6. 3, 2, 7, 9, 5, 10
7. 7900 + 91 500 = 99 400
8. 2361 cm
9. 98 201 tonnes
10. $5570
11. 1100, 11 000
12. 30, 10
13. 90, 80
14. $3\frac{3}{4}$ apples each
15. 109 000
16. −4 °C
17. $413.55, $29.70, $821.40
18. $1.50
19. 23.6 kg
20. 1795.42
21. 41 400, 62 650, 74 800
22. add 0.03

Unit 20B page 59

1. 1 134 683
2. 79 998 g
3. 540 000, 180 000, 270 000
4. true
5. $\frac{13}{12} = 1\frac{1}{12}$
6. 36
7. 260
8. 0105
9. 3:20 pm
10. 9.4 L
11. A (A has a perimeter of 32 m and B of 28 m.)
12. $>$
13. 8, 16, 24, 32
14. circle
15.
16. parent/carer to check
17. 55°
18. 40%
19. 50% or $\frac{1}{2}$ or 0.5
20. 6
21. $\frac{1}{4}$
22. dance

Unit 21A page 60

1. 115, 126, 171, 136, 158, 142
2. 64, 60, 78, 36, 27, 49
3. 2, 18, 10, 16, 22, 6
4. 44, 77, 22, 66, 132, 110
5. 7, 10, 3, 1, 6, 9
6. 4, 3, 6, 8, 5, 12
7. $58 661, $58 583
8. 1 554 303
9. $8280
10. 8570 − 723 = 7847
11. 140, 280, 420
12. 800
13. $140\frac{1}{3}$
14. 72
15. parent/carer to check
16. 132
17. $5
18. $55.87
19. 2.3
20. 32 m
21. 432 500, 869 100
22. 360, 650

Answers

Unit 21B page 61

1. 180 000
2. 41 309
3. 12 240
4. $5786\frac{3}{8}$ or 5786 r 3
5. **A** $\frac{6}{10} = \frac{3}{5}$

   B $\frac{91}{100}$

   C $\frac{3}{100}$
6. $\frac{3}{4}$
7. 12, 12
8. 
9. 4.10 or 10 past 4
10. 400 mm
11. A 18 cm^2, B 20 cm^2, Answer B
12. 10.5 kg or 10 500 g
13. false
14. square
15. rotation
16. 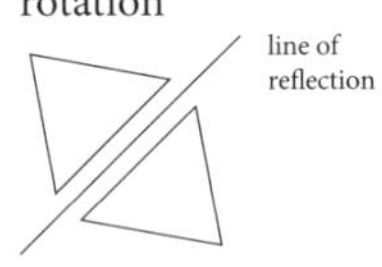

17. 150°
18. 24
19. 360
20.

Shape	Number
triangle	8
circle	9
square	5

21. 40
22. parent/carer to check

Unit 22A page 62

1. 106, 140, 85, 155, 162, 117
2. 43, 2, 13, 49, 24, 40
3. 14, 6, 20, 4, 24, 16
4. 11, 121, 55, 99, 44, 66
5. 2, 7, 4, 12, 1, 9
6. 10, 1, 9, 7, 3, 12
7. $366 504, $164 409
8. 1 017 687
9. $1750
10. 8100 – 6906 = 1194
11. 750, 1500, 2250
12. 1800
13. $141\frac{5}{6}$
14. 54
15. parent/carer to check
16. 261
17. $8
18. $301.76
19. 1.22
20. 12.5 L
21. 610 600, 621 100
22. 370, 130

Unit 22B page 63

1. 160 000
2. 136
3. 19 920
4. 9954
5. **A** $\frac{9}{10}$

   B $\frac{85}{100}$ or $\frac{17}{20}$

   C $\frac{6}{100}$ or $\frac{3}{50}$
6. $\frac{5}{6}$ of a bag
7. 7, 7
8. 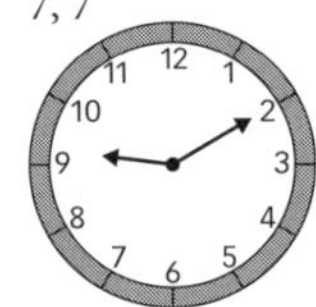
9. 5 o'clock (5:00)
10. 9.1 kg
11. A 24 cm^2, B 28 cm^2, Answer B
12. 2502 mL (2.502 L)
13. true
14. triangles
15. reflection
16. line of reflection
17. 60°
18. 26
19. 400
20.

Shape	Number
star	10
heart	7
triangle	7

21. 25
22. parent/carer to check

Unit 23A page 64

1. 142, 158, 185, 118, 165, 146
2. 47, 26, 41, 61, 28, 7
3. 12, 0, 18, 6, 20, 8
4. 22, 88, 55, 121, 77, 11
5. 11, 1, 7, 3, 4, 9
6. 12, 6, 3, 5, 1, 11
7. $127 960, $430 512
8. 1 172 085
9. $2290
10. 8563 – 2408 = 6155
11. 330, 660, 990
12. 800
13. 145
14. 75
15. parent/carer to check
16. 30
17. $11
18. $91.10
19. 2.7
20. 42 m
21. 439 600, 711 400
22. 590, 440

Unit 23B page 65

1. 180 000
2. 4894
3. 14 112
4. $6959\frac{3}{5}$ or 6959 r 3
5. **A** $1\frac{6}{10}$ $(1\frac{3}{5})$

   B $\frac{3}{100}$

   C $\frac{45}{100}$ $(\frac{9}{20})$
6. $\frac{3}{10}$
7. 11, 7
8. 
9. 4:35
10. 31 mL
11. A 30 m^2, B 36 m^2, Answer B
12. 4.3 kg or 4300 g
13. true
14. triangle, rectangle
15. rotation
16. 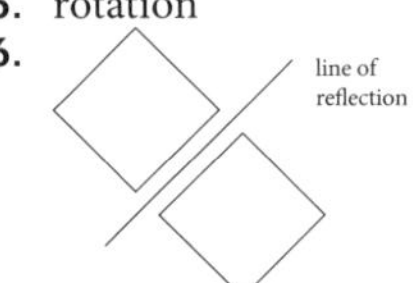

17. 100°
18. 10
19. 260
20.

Fruit	Number
apple	5
pear	7
pineapple	10

21. 200
22. parent/carer to check

Revision 3A page 66

1. 75, 101, 97, 83, 69, 50
2. 11, 52, 36, 79, 25, 81
3. 8, 44, 20, 32, 36, 12
4. 66, 11, 110, 77, 132, 44
5. 10, 1, 6, 9, 3, 12
6. 7, 6, 9, 8, 3, 12
7. $41 041
8. 1292 km
9. 16 798 cm
10. 6528 + 2876 = 9404
11. 120, 1200, 12 000
12. 4, 48
13. B
14. 54
15. D
16. C
17. $3
18. B
19. 24 m
20. 2.24
21. 149 900
22. 590

Revision 3B page 67

1. 210 000
2. 3700
3. 13 500
4. true
5. C
6. $\frac{2}{5}$
7. 9
8. 
9. 4:10 or 10 past 4
10. B
11. B
12. <
13. *AB*
14. A, B
15. C
16. 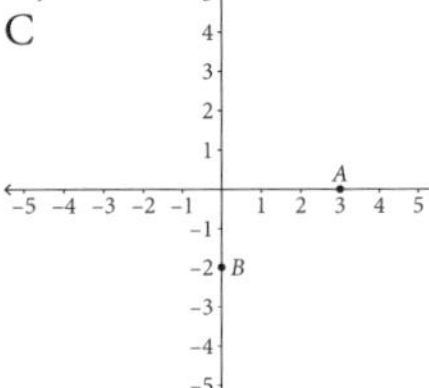
17. 55°
18. 10%
19. 26
20. 4
21. $\frac{1}{4}$
22. bacon

NAPLAN-style Test 3 pages 68–71

1. B
2. 71 km
3. A
4. A
5. 77
6. B
7. D
8. C
9. 19.5
10. C
11. A
12. B
13. A
14. B
15. B
16. B
17. D
18. B
19. B
20. square

Unit 24A page 72

1. 117, 132, 86, 100, 112, 138
2. 62, 45, 23, 34, 12, 4
3. 2, 12, 14, 8, 24, 18
4. 55, 88, 22, 110, 121, 33
5. 10, 4, 2, 3, 7, 1
6. 11, 1, 5, 3, 6, 10
7. $53 054, $784 629

Answers

8. 2 100 048
9. $31 300
10. 5118 – 4814 = 304
11. 520, 1040, 1560
12. 600
13. $103\frac{1}{2}$
14. 80
15. parent/carer to check
16. 129
17. $9
18. $77.53
19. 1.9
20. 17.5 kg
21. 496 300, 791 100
22. 280, 680

Unit 24B page 73

1. 190 000
2. 59 993
3. 9672
4. 4759
5. A $2\frac{1}{2}$ or $2\frac{5}{10}$
   B $1\frac{6}{100}$ ($1\frac{3}{50}$)
   C $1\frac{91}{100}$
6. $\frac{1}{4}$
7. 9, 9
8. 
9. 5:05 or 5 past 5
10. 400 m
11. 40 m^2, 42 m^2, Answer B
12. 7.9 L or 7900 mL
13. false
14. circle, rectangle
15. translation
16.
17. 170°
18. 16
19. 240
20.

Item	Number
bowl	7
cup	6
plate	5

21. 180
22. parent/carer to check

Unit 25A page 74

1. 116, 118, 140, 94, 99, 151
2. 61, 22, 9, 34, 46, 13
3. 12, 4, 16, 8, 18, 24
4. 11, 110, 33, 55, 121, 77
5. 9, 1, 6, 3, 8, 4
6. 10, 6, 2, 8, 4, 12
7. $233 797, $178 877

8. 1 501 743
9. $37 900
10. 5159 – 3127 = 2032
11. 870, 1740, 2610
12. 2100
13. $45\frac{3}{5}$
14. 167
15. parent/carer to check
16. 183
17. $21
18. $233.21
19. 1.4
20. 31 m
21. 183 100, 798 500
22. 190, 290

Unit 25B page 75

1. 190 000
2. 90 316
3. 34 248
4. 9121
5. A $6\frac{3}{10}$
   B $\frac{5}{100}$ ($\frac{1}{20}$)
   C $\frac{8}{10}$ ($\frac{4}{5}$)
6. $\frac{7}{12}$
7. 6, 6
8. 
9. 3:55
10. 90 s
11. 56 m^2 54 m^2 Answer A
12. 9.3 kg or 9300 g
13. true
14. square, triangle
15. rotation
16. 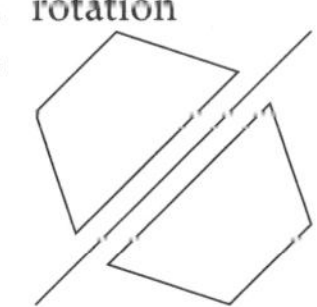
17. 90°
18. 14
19. 240
20.

Item	Number
flower	7
straw	8
shovel	7

21. 50
22. parent/carer to check

Unit 26A page 76

1. 1.7, 4.5, 6.3, 8.4, 3.5, 2.6
2. 6, 9.2, 8.3, 7.5, 2.6, 3.4
3. 12, 48, 36, 84, 132, 108
4. 30, 12, 48, 60, 72, 36
5. 12, 1, 5, 4, 2, 10
6. 12, 2, 8, 5, 4, 11
7. 3552 + 1278 = 4830

8. 11 903
9. 945 474
10. 629
11. 3126
12. 32 000
13. 2468
14. 3705
15. 4 + 25 = 29
16. 109 000
17. $54
18. $103.10, $69.70
19. 7.3
20. 1.63
21. $56 000, $85 000
22. 120, 40

Unit 26B page 77

1. 123 585
2. 17 725
3. 419 010
4. 617 r 2
5.

Decimal	Fraction	Percentage
0.9	$\frac{9}{10}$	90%
0.4	$\frac{4}{10}$	40%
0.16	$\frac{16}{100}$	16%

6. <
7. 5
8. 6:10
9. 1 hour and 15 minutes
10. 6.2 kg or 6200 g
11. A = 30 m^2 P = 30 m
12. 18
13. cone
14. 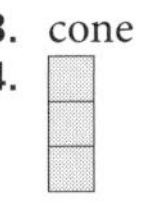
15. 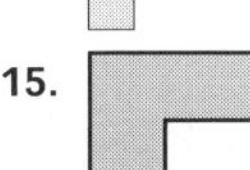
16. 12 units^2
17. 4
18. $\frac{5}{10}$ or $\frac{1}{2}$
19. parent/carer to check
20. 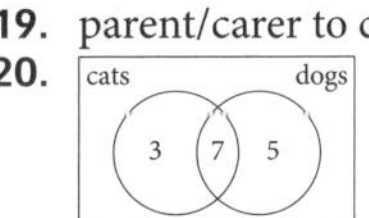

21. 1.5 million
22. between 2000 and 2010

Unit 27A page 78

1. 6.6, 10.2, 9.4, 6.8, 3.6, 6.0
2. 2.5, 5.3, 5.7, 7.6, 3.4, 7.1
3. 12, 84, 36, 144, 108, 60
4. 24, 60, 12, 48, 66, 36
5. 3, 7, 10, 4, 11, 6
6. 10, 3, 11, 4, 12, 9
7. 3248 + 4763 = 8011
8. 8122
9. 204 158
10. 1517
11. 4473
12. 54 000
13. 364
14. 7440

15. 49 – 9 = 40
16. – 4 °C
17. $90
18. $4116.95, $9121.50
19. 8.4
20. 1.59
21. $52 000, $19 000
22. 120, 80

Unit 27B page 79

1. 78 776
2. 78 509
3. 329 819
4. 936
5.

Decimal	Fraction	Percentage
0.8	$\frac{4}{5}$	80%
0.2	$\frac{2}{10}$ ($\frac{1}{5}$)	20%
0.3	$\frac{3}{10}$	30%

6. >
7. 6
8. 10:00 pm
9. 1 hour 20 minutes
10. 2.815 kg or 2815 g
11. A = 40 cm^2 P = 26 cm
12. 40
13. cylinder
14.
15.
16. 30 units^2
17. 5
18. $\frac{5}{10} = \frac{1}{2}$
19. parent/carer to check
20. 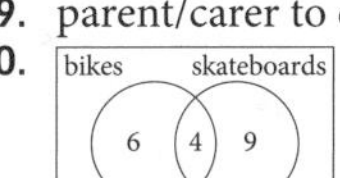

21. 30 °C
22. 15 °C

Unit 28A page 80

1. 7.9, 5.7, 10.5, 5.4, 7.3, 8.8
2. 2.3, 3.9, 2.2, 5.9, 5, 3.8
3. 48, 72, 108, 24, 120, 132
4. 21, 56, 7, 49, 84, 35
5. 7, 10, 3, 6, 5, 8
6. 10, 2, 4, 8, 1, 12
7. 6914 + 2836 = 9750
8. 10 308
9. 694 071
10. 1653
11. 2884
12. 56 000
13. 685
14. 10 863
15. 25 + 16 = 41
16. 0 °C
17. $16.25
18. $666.25, $8919.90
19. 8.95
20. 7.98
21. $89 000, $42 000
22. 40, 50

Answers

Unit 28B page 81

1. 152 222
2. 65 618
3. 70 803
4. 1076
5.

Decimal	Fraction	Percentage
0.8	$\frac{8}{10}$ $(\frac{4}{5})$	80%
0.15	$\frac{15}{100}$ $(\frac{3}{20})$	15%
0.25	$\frac{1}{4}$	25%

6. <
7. 200
8. 6:15 pm
9. 1 hour 5 minutes
10. 2.8 kg or 2800 g
11. A = 60 cm² P = 40 cm
12. 40
13. octagonal-based pyramid
14. 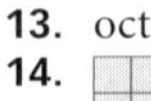
15. 
16. 15 units²
17. 6
18. $\frac{2}{10} = \frac{1}{5}$
19. parent/carer to check
20. 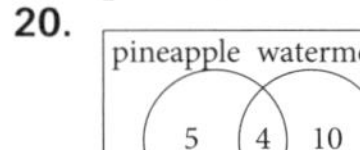

21. 1.6 m
22. 40 cm or 0.4 m

Unit 29A page 82

1. 11.6, 13.2, 8.3, 7.2, 12.8, 9.9
2. 1.6, 3.2, 5.5, 7.3, 5.1, 3
3. 12, 48, 120, 84, 144, 36
4. 25, 45, 55, 40, 10, 30
5. 10, 1, 4, 9, 3, 12
6. 1, 6, 9, 5, 7, 10
7. 2917 + 4939 = 7856
8. 17 624
9. 50 750
10. 1359
11. 2282
12. 30 000
13. 798
14. 16 926
15. 100 – 9 = 91
16. 7 °C
17. $24.45
18. $6121.85, $72 120.65
19. 11.3
20. 16.49
21. $2000, $4000
22. 120, 200

Unit 29B page 83

1. 125 600
2. 73 820
3. 210 550
4. 238
5.

Decimal	Fraction	Percentage
0.2	$\frac{2}{10}$ $(\frac{1}{5})$	20%
0.4	$\frac{4}{10}$ $(\frac{2}{5})$	40%
0.17	$\frac{17}{100}$	17%

6. <
7. 87
8. 5:30 pm
9. 1 hour 25 minutes
10. 2.1 kg or 2100 g
11. A = 60 cm² P = 32 m
12. 36
13. hexagonal prism
14. 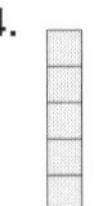
15. 
16. 32 units²
17. 4
18. 0
19. parent/carer to check
20. 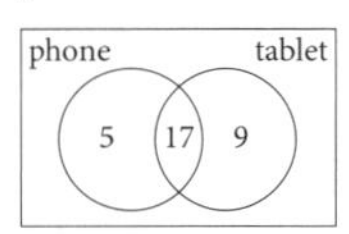

21. $50 000
22. $10 000

Unit 30A page 84

1. 5.3, 9.9, 13.4, 6.2, 8, 9.1
2. 1.1, 2.7, 3.2, 6, 7.5, 4.9
3. 12, 108, 60, 132, 84, 24
4. 36, 60, 18, 72, 48, 24
5. 10, 8, 3, 1, 7, 12
6. 12, 7, 9, 5, 3, 10
7. 8914 + 2638 = 11 552
8. 13 586
9. 252 952
10. 2440
11. 2108
12. 36 000
13. 693
14. 13 862
15. 9 + 16 = 25
16. –4 °C
17. $660
18. $4190.70, $63 235.85
19. 9.66
20. 38.92
21. $4000, $9000
22. 80, 40

Unit 30B page 85

1. 106 217
2. 17 209
3. 333 417
4. 175
5.

Decimal	Fraction	Percentage
1.5	$1\frac{1}{2}$	150%
0.4	$\frac{2}{5}$	40%
0.7	$\frac{7}{10}$	70%

6. <
7. 116
8. 8:15 pm
9. 1 hour 5 minutes
10. 8650 g or 8.65 kg
11. A = 6 cm² P = 12 cm
12. 28
13. pentagonal prism
14. 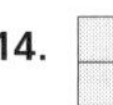
15. 
16. 6 unit²
17. 4
18. $\frac{5}{10} = \frac{1}{2}$
19. parent/carer to check
20. 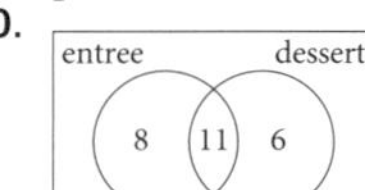

21. 50 km
22. 100 km

Revision 4A page 86

1. 7.3, 10.5, 9.6, 5.7, 8.9, 7.1
2. 2.4, 4, 5.6, 2.3, 1.1, 4.5
3. 48, 96, 12, 108, 132, 36
4. 30, 50, 10, 25, 60, 35
5. 12, 1, 6, 5, 2, 10
6. 1, 4, 10, 5, 11, 12
7. 3965 + 1479 = 5444
8. 13 785
9. 938 525 m
10. 1328
11. 4815
12. 8, 40
13. A
14. $6\frac{1}{4}$ oranges
15. D
16. 249
17. $13
18. $170.68
19. 1.7
20. 12.6 m
21. 69 089 100
22. 330

Revision 4B page 87

1. 190 000
2. 33 869
3. 445 686
4. 568
5.

Decimal	Fraction	Percentage
0.6	$\frac{6}{10}$ $(\frac{3}{5})$	60%
0.2	$\frac{1}{5}$	20%
0.1	$\frac{1}{10}$	10%

6. >
7. 15
8. 11:40 pm
9. 1 hour 45 minutes
10. C
11. A
12. 27 cm³
13. rectangular prism
14. triangles
15. 
16. 24 units²
17. C
18. 50% or $\frac{5}{10}$ $(\frac{1}{2})$
19. 260
20. basketball: 9, both: 10, soccer: 6
21. 20 °C
22. 5

NAPLAN-style Test 4 pages 88–92

1. D
2. A
3. 6344
4. A
5. D
6. $30
7. D
8. C
9. B
10. B
11. A
12. 16 370 drawing pins
13. $\frac{6}{100}$ $(\frac{3}{50})$, 6%
14. D
15. <
16. C
17. C
18. A
19. 20 units
20. C

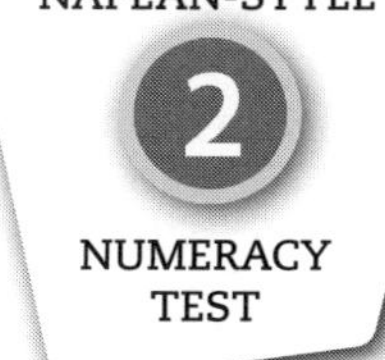

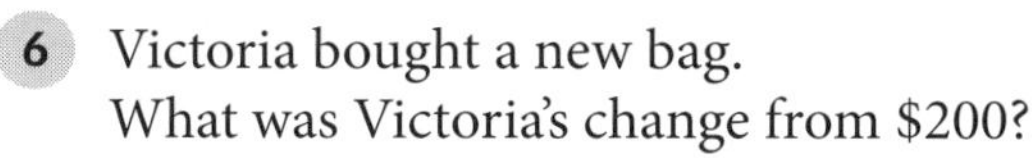

6 Victoria bought a new bag.
What was Victoria's change from $200?

A $21
B $31
C $41
D $141

7 This book is on sale for 50% off the normal price.
What is the book's sale price?

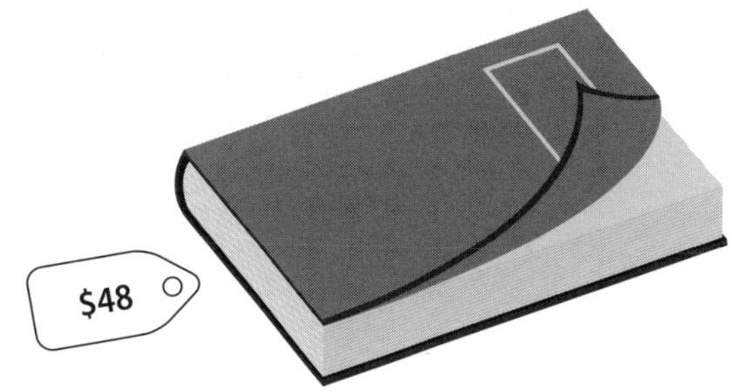

Sale price: ☐

8 What is the difference between 8.07 and 4.92?

A 3.15
B 3.19
C 4.95
D 4.99

9 What is a description of the number pattern?

3, 4.5, 6, 7.5

A add 1.5
B subtract 0.5
C multiply 1.5
D divide 2

10 Noha needs to pick 3 cards to make 1000.
Her first 2 cards are:

365 249

Which is the third card Noha should pick?

386	416	506	614
A	B	C	D

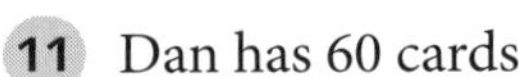

11 Dan has 60 cards.

He needs to give $\frac{1}{5}$ of them to his teacher.

How many cards does Dan give to his teacher?

A 5
B 10
C 12
D 20

12

3 hours = ☐ minutes

13 A plane leaves at 17:25. What time is this in am/pm time?

A 2:25 pm
B 4:25 pm
C 5:25 pm
D 7:25 pm

14 What is the perimeter of this shape?

P = ☐

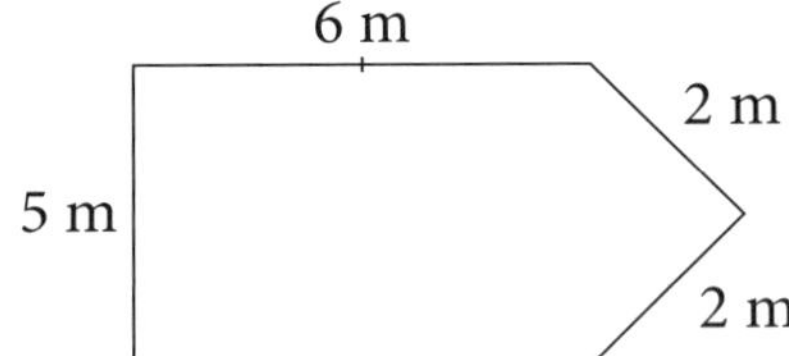

15 Which bottle has the most?

A

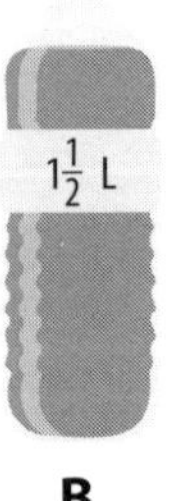

B

C

D

16 Draw the triangle rotated $\frac{1}{4}$ turn anticlockwise.

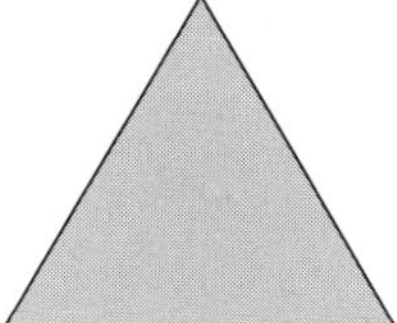

17 Rachel is estimating the size of the angle.
What is the best estimate?

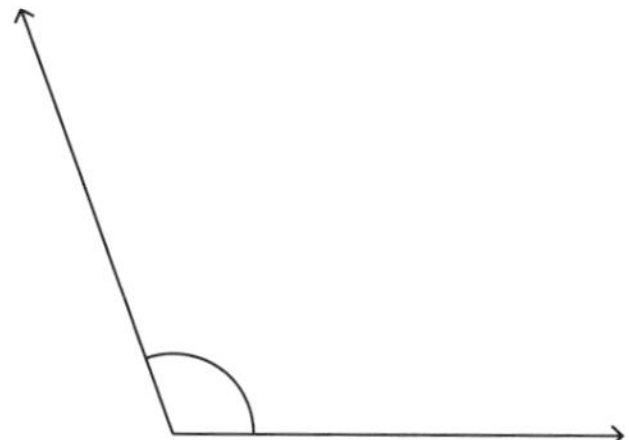

A 70°
B 90°
C 110°
D 170°

18 The spinner is spun to start the game. A 6 is needed to start.
What is the chance of spinning a 6?

A $\frac{1}{6}$

B $\frac{1}{4}$

C $\frac{1}{2}$

D 1

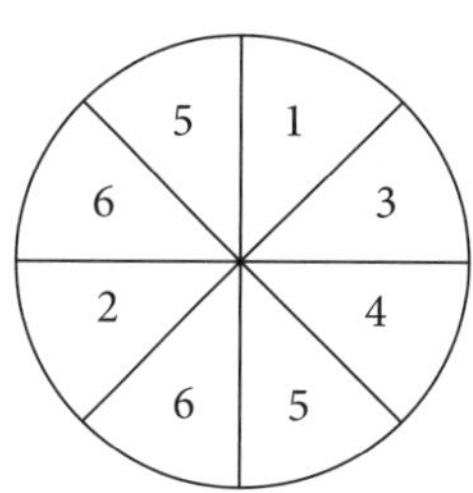

19 The types of vehicles sold was recorded.

Vehicle	Number sold
car	15
boat	6
motorbike	3
van	7

Which type of vehicle had the least sold?

20 The number of pets adopted from a shelter was recorded.
How many more dogs were adopted than rabbits?

A 5
B 20
C 25
D 30

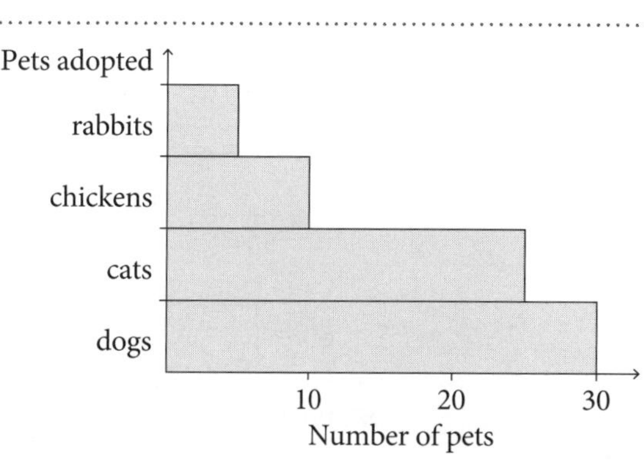

1

+	47	61	36	52	10	28
20						

2

–	97	71	46	64	50	83
10						

3

×	3	10	5	12	8	2
4						

4

×	6	11	1	9	7	4
10						

5

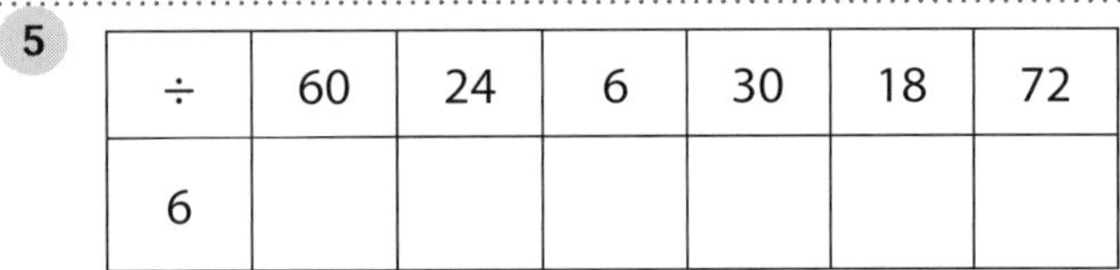

÷	60	24	6	30	18	72
6						

6

÷	81	36	72	18	54	9
9						

7 Estimate by first rounding each number to the nearest hundred.

$3876 + 2281 = \square$

8 What is the total length?

$463\text{ m} + 194\text{ m} + 221\text{ m} = \square$

9

$$\begin{array}{r} 875\,926\text{ kg} \\ -\ \ 321\,101\text{ kg} \\ \hline \end{array}$$

10 What is the difference between $4500 and $7950?

11

$7 \times 60 = \square$

$7 \times 600 = \square$

12 Complete the boxes.

$\square \times 3 = \square = 6 \times 4$

13

$180 \div 3 = \square$

$240 \div 6 = \square$

14 How much would 5 children receive if they shared 12 pieces of fruit equally?

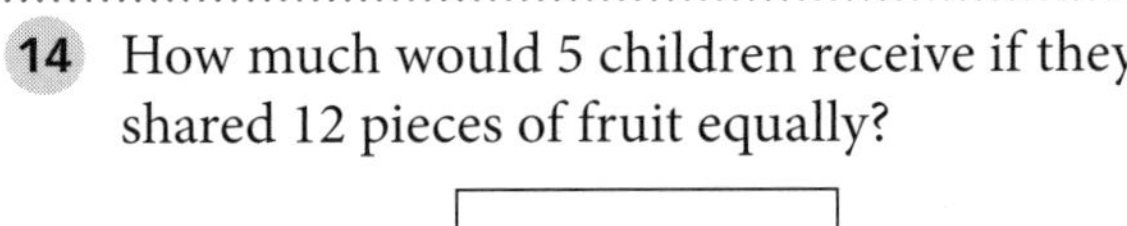

15 Circle the smallest number.

427 000   378 000   109 000   423 000

16 What is 5 °C less than the temperature shown?

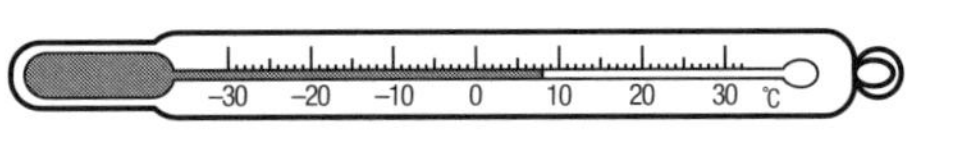

17 Round each of the following to the nearest 5c.

$23.47 ☐ $48.52 ☐ $66.39 ☐

18 Find 10% of $3.00.

19 Alex has 4 lengths of wood. Each length of wood is 3.64 m long. What is the total length of wood altogether?

20 Find the total of 26.39, 17.56 and 19.02.

21 Round each number to the nearest 50.

13 847 ☐   49 621 ☐   77 418 ☐

22 What is the rule for this pattern?

6.3, 6.6, 6.9, 7.2

1

$$\begin{array}{r} 247\,983 \\ 109\,725 \\ +\ \ 83\,609 \\ \hline \end{array}$$

2 The lightest flying bird weighs 1.6 g and the heaviest flying bird weighs 21 000 g. What is the difference between the weights of the two birds?

3 Complete:

×	40 000	80 000	90 000
6			

4 True or false?

78 720 ÷ 8 = 9840

5 Sarah added together the two fractions written on the cards. What was the answer?

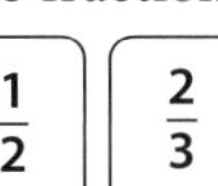

6 There were 12 apples in a bag. Jack ate $\frac{1}{3}$ of the apples. How many apples did Jack eat?

7 Sophie has 11 cards. Cindy has 8 cards more than Sophie. How many cards does Cindy need to give Sophie for them to have the same number of cards?

8 Write 7:55 pm as 24-hour time.

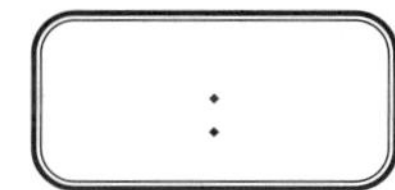

9 It is 4:10 pm. Jack's karate class goes for 70 minutes. What time does the class finish?

10

9500 mL = ☐ L

11 Which rectangle has the longer perimeter?

	Length	Width	Perimeter
A	2 cm	3 cm	
B	1 cm	5 cm	

12 Complete with >, < or =.

0.4 kg ☐ 4000 g

13 Complete the table.

Number of triangles	1	2	3	4
Number of sides				

14 Draw the top view of:

15 Continue the pattern.

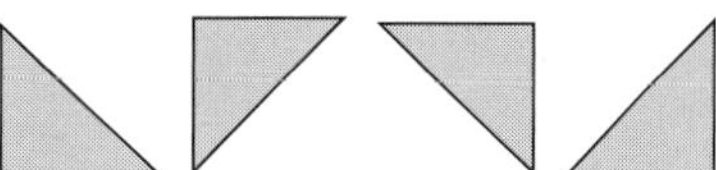

16 Draw and label the two points on the coordinate axes.

A (3, 1)

B (−2, −2)

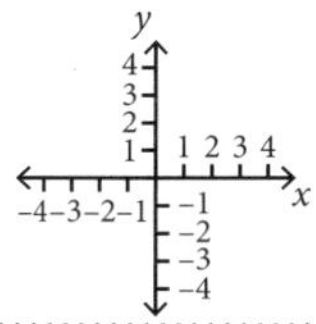

17 What is the value of *a*?

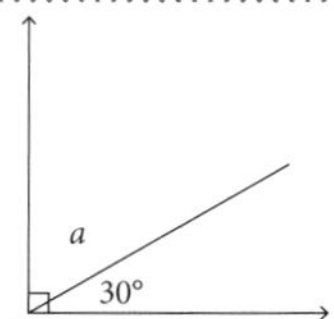

18 Joe has a $\frac{1}{10}$ chance of selecting a green card. What is this as a percentage?

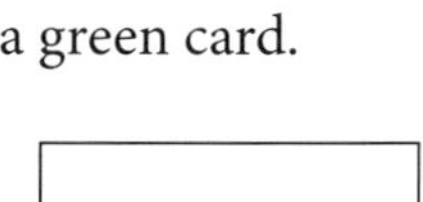

19 What is the chance of getting a head when flipping one coin?

20 How many students don't have a dog or a cat?

	Has a dog	Doesn't have a dog
Has a cat	6	3
Doesn't have a cat	9	7

21 What fraction of people have a bike?

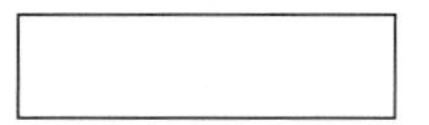

22 Which vehicle has the smallest amount?

bike | truck | car

1

+	41	26	10	39	53	17
30						

2

–	96	71	53	44	60	85
20						

3

×	1	12	5	7	10	3
4						

4

×	6	11	2	9	8	4
10						

5

÷	6	42	12	66	54	36
6						

6

÷	9	36	54	63	90	108
9						

7 Estimate by first rounding each number to the nearest hundred.

$4979 + 9312 = \square$

8 What is the total length?

674 cm + 393 cm + 847 cm = ☐

9

873 925 m
− 146 342 m

10 What is the difference between \$3250 and \$6920?

☐

11

$8 \times 50 = \square$

$8 \times 500 = \square$

12 Complete the boxes.

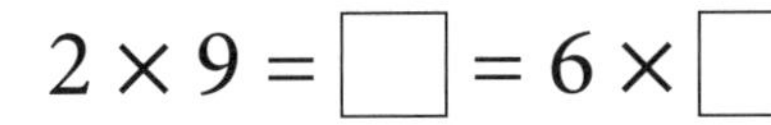

$2 \times 9 = \square = 6 \times \square$

13

$400 \div 8 = \square$

$360 \div 9 = \square$

14 How much would 7 parents receive if they shared 18 pieces of cake equally?

☐

15 Circle the smallest number.

670 000 721 000 940 000 852 000

16 What is 7 °C less than the temperature shown? ☐

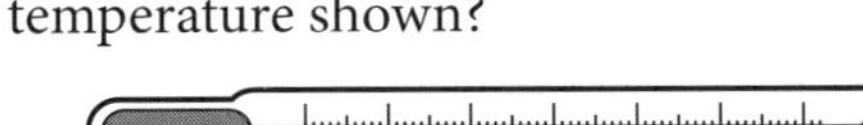

17 Round each of the following to the nearest 5c.

\$33.46 ☐ \$118.01 ☐ \$213.79 ☐

18 Find 10% of \$9.00.

☐

19 Taylor has 6 pieces of ribbon. Each piece of ribbon is 1.63 m long. What is the total length of the ribbon altogether?

☐

20 Find the total of 18.25, 26.7 and 39.31.

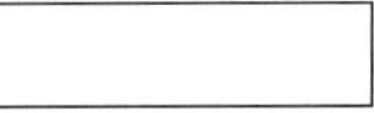

21 Round each number to the nearest 50.

24 763 ☐ 78 506 ☐ 69 395 ☐

22 What is the rule for this pattern?

5.11, 5.22, 5.33, 5.44

1

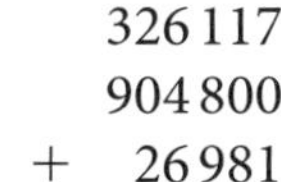

$$\begin{array}{r} 326\,117 \\ 904\,800 \\ +\ \ 26\,981 \\ \hline \end{array}$$

2 The albatross has a wingspan of 300 cm and the hummingbird has a wingspan of 3.25 cm. What is the difference between the wingspans of the two birds?

3 Complete:

×	30 000	50 000	70 000
7			

4 True or false?

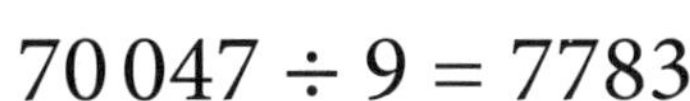

$70\,047 \div 9 = 7783$

5 Max added together the fractions on the two cards. What was the answer?

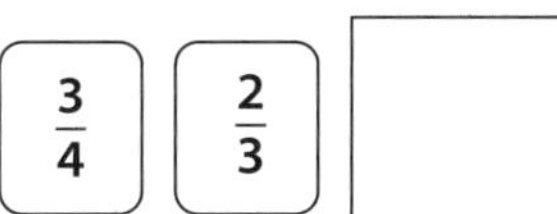

6 Lily had a box of 24 pencils. She gave away $\frac{1}{4}$ of the pencils. How many pencils did Lily have left?

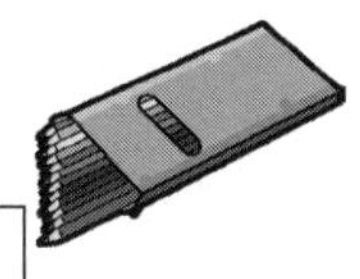

7 San has 11 pencils. Che has 6 pencils more than San. Isla has 7 more pencils than Che. How many pencils are there altogether?

8 Write 10:10 pm as 24-hour time.

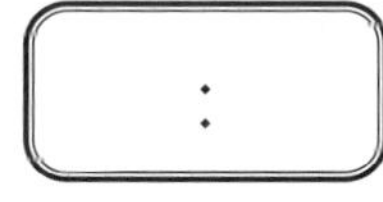

9 Sara's horseriding lesson starts at 4:40 pm. It goes for 80 minutes. What time does the lesson finish?

10

$6\text{ L} = \square\text{ mL}$

11 Which rectangle has the longer perimeter?

	Length	Width	Perimeter
A	4 cm	3 cm	
B	5 cm	2 cm	

12 Complete with >, < or =.

$9\text{ kg} \square 8000\text{ g}$

13 Complete the table.

Number of squares	1	2	3	4
Number of sides				

14 Draw the top view of:

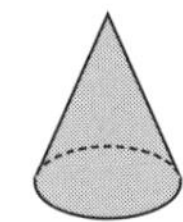

15 Continue the pattern.

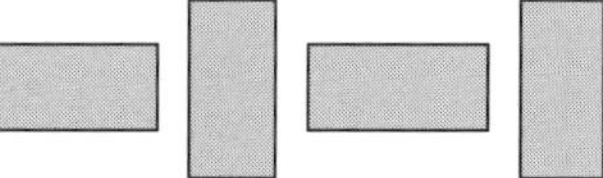

16 Draw and label the two points on the coordinate axes.
C (4, 2)
D (−2, 3)

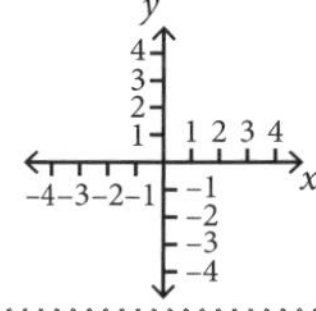

17 What is the value of a?

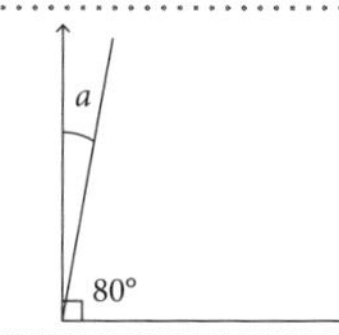

18 Kenny has a $\frac{7}{10}$ chance of selecting a green card.

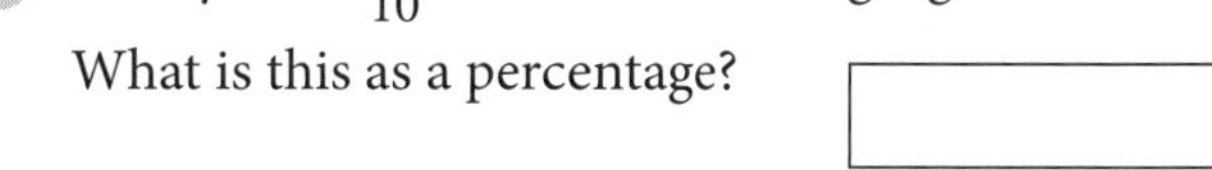

What is this as a percentage?

19 What is the chance as a percentage of getting a tail when flipping one coin?

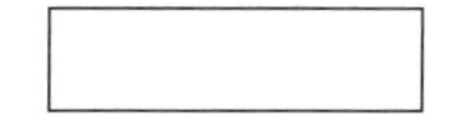

20 How many students have both a bike and a scooter?

	Has a scooter	Doesn't have a scooter
Has a bike	15	12
Doesn't have a bike	3	2

21 What fraction of people like grapes or oranges?

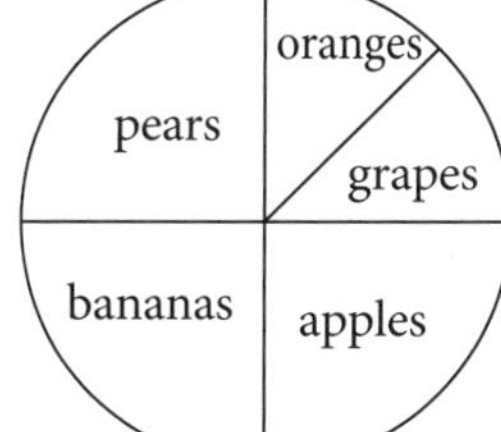

22 What fraction of people like apples more than oranges?

UNIT 18A

1

+	21	42	19	28	36	7
40						

2

–	46	52	96	81	60	39
30						

3

×	4	9	2	8	10	5
4						

4

×	6	11	1	7	12	3
10						

5

÷	6	60	48	54	72	36
6						

6

÷	18	90	45	99	72	27
9						

7 Estimate by first rounding each number to the nearest hundred.

61 370 + 7496 = ☐

8 What is the total length?

969 mm + 485 mm + 897 mm = ☐

9

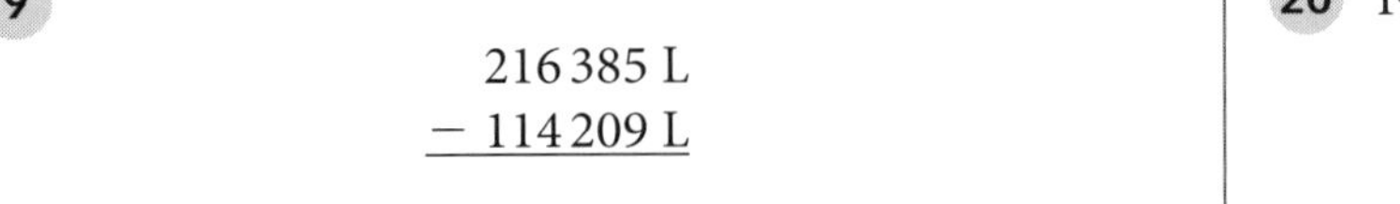

216 385 L
− 114 209 L

10 What is the difference between $4730 and $8560?

11

9 × 20 = ☐

9 × 200 = ☐

12 Complete the boxes.

5 × ☐ = ☐ = 10 × 2

13

720 ÷ 6 = ☐

800 ÷ 10 = ☐

14 How much would 7 football players receive if they shared 25 oranges equally?

☐

15 Circle the smallest number.

176 000 462 000 381 000 479 000

16 What is 3 °C more than the temperature shown? ☐

–30 –20 –10 0 10 20 30 °C

17 Round each of the following to the nearest 5c.

$74.31 ☐ $819.63 ☐ $117.54 ☐

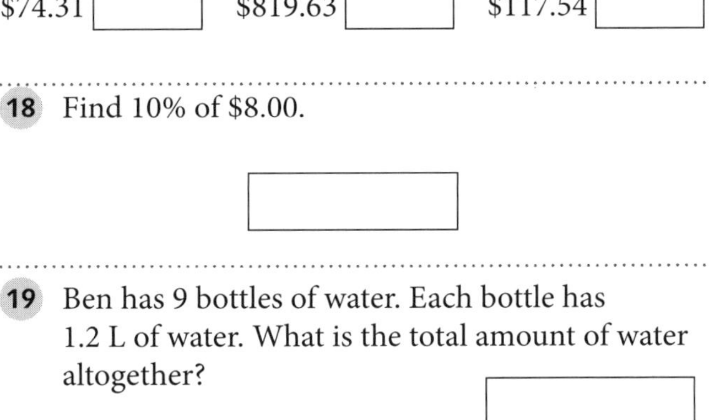

18 Find 10% of $8.00.

☐

19 Ben has 9 bottles of water. Each bottle has 1.2 L of water. What is the total amount of water altogether?

☐

20 Find the total of 411.63, 312.85 and 29.9.

☐

21 Round each number to the nearest 50.

61 163 ☐ 71 409 ☐ 92 183 ☐

22 What is the rule for this pattern?

10.04, 10.08, 10.12, 10.16

☐

1

$$\begin{array}{r} 806\,385 \\ 97\,117 \\ +\ \ 463\,108 \\ \hline \end{array}$$

2 A blue whale weighs 140 000 kg. A baby blue whale weighs 3000 kg. What is the difference between the weights of the two whales?

3 Complete:

×	90 000	70 000	40 000
5			

4 True or false?

35 865 ÷ 5 = 8965

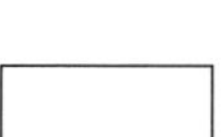

5 Andrew added together the fractions on the two cards. What was the answer?

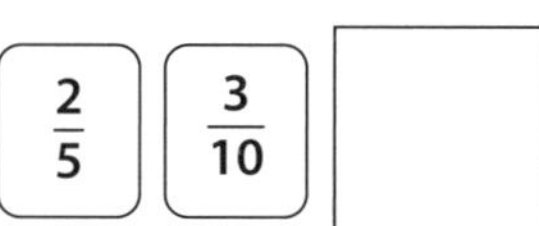

6 There were 50 flowers in buckets. Doreen sold $\frac{3}{10}$ of the flowers. How many flowers did Doreen sell?

7 Bread rolls come in different-sized packets. There are 6 bread rolls in each of 8 packets and 12 rolls in each of 4 packets. How many bread rolls are there altogether?

8 Write 8:05 pm as 24-hour time.

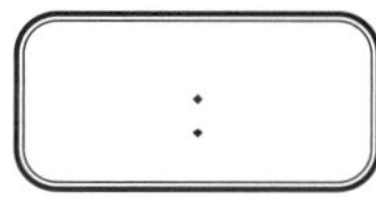

9 Luis's piano lesson starts at 3:15 pm. It goes for 90 minutes. What time does the lesson finish?

10

7500 mL = ☐ L

11 Which rectangle has the longer perimeter?

	Length	Width	Perimeter
A	7 cm	4 cm	
B	8 cm	3 cm	

12 Complete with >, < or =.

13 Complete the table.

Number of rectangles	1	2	3	4
Number of sides				

14 Draw the top view of:

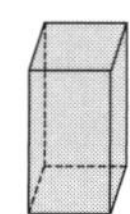

15 Continue the pattern.

16 Draw and label the two points on the coordinate axes.
A (−5, 2)
B (−1, 0)

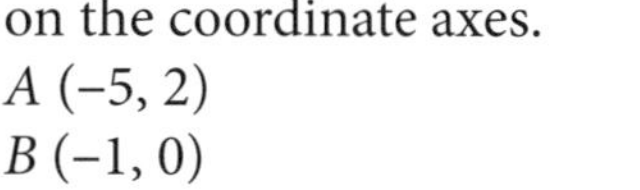

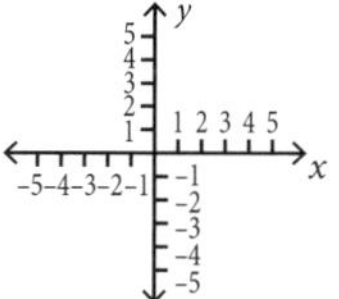

17 What is the value of *a*?

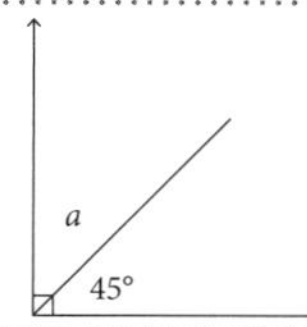

18 Belle has a $\frac{9}{10}$ chance of **not** selecting an orange card. What is this as a percentage?

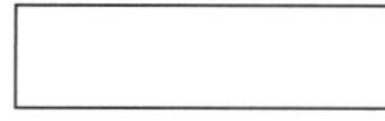

19 What is the chance of getting 2 tails when flipping 2 coins?

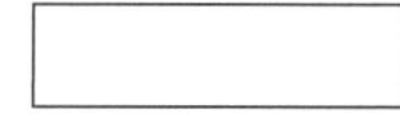

20 How many people like the beach and the mountains?

	Likes the mountains	Doesn't like the mountains
Likes the beach	20	16
Doesn't like the beach	14	12

21 What is/are the most popular colour(s)?

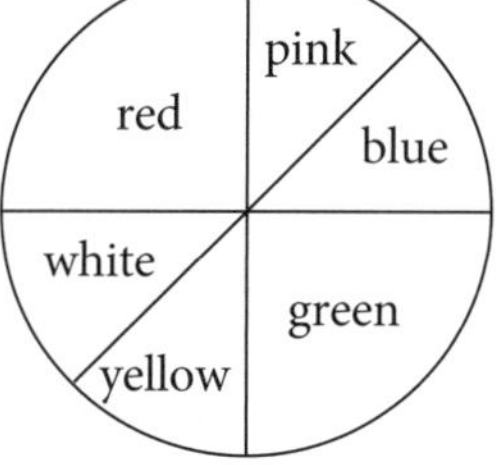

22 What fraction of people like white or blue?

1

+	7	40	27	51	35	19
50						

2

–	81	63	50	79	98	100
40						

3

×	2	12	6	7	9	4
4						

4

×	10	5	3	11	1	8
10						

5

÷	54	30	66	24	36	72
6						

6

÷	99	45	81	108	63	27
9						

7 Estimate by first rounding each number to the nearest hundred.

72 365 + 29 471 = ☐

8 What is the total length?

812 km + 956 km + 772 km = ☐

9

  873 146 m
− 243 105 m

10 What is the difference between $1990 and $4800?

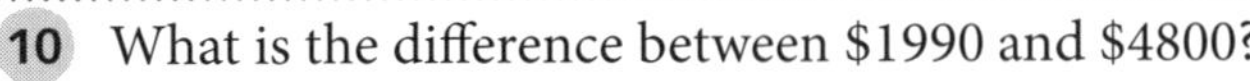

☐

11

4 × 80 = ☐

4 × 800 = ☐

12 Complete the boxes.

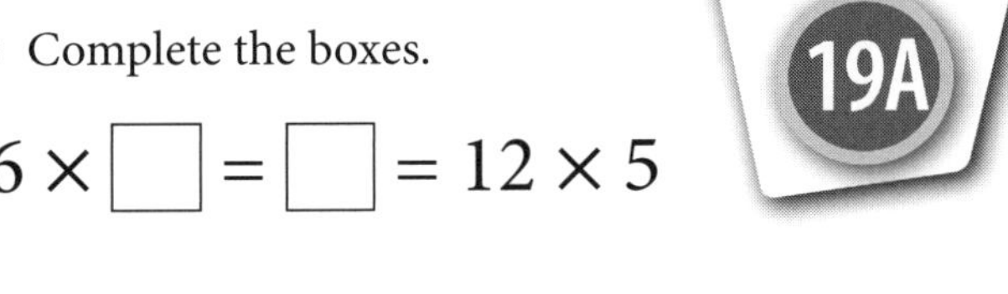

6 × ☐ = ☐ = 12 × 5

13

350 ÷ 7 = ☐

420 ÷ 6 = ☐

14 How much would 7 teachers receive if they shared 30 chocolate bars equally?

☐

15 Circle the smallest number.

476 000   923 000   385 000   201 000

16 What is 8 °C more than the temperature shown?

☐

–30 –20 –10 0 10 20 30 °C

17 Round each of the following to the nearest 5c.

$412.96 ☐ $612.61 ☐ $98.19 ☐

18 Find 10% of $11.00.

☐

19 Jess has 7 pieces of material. Each piece is 3.21 m long. What is the total length of material altogether?

☐

20 Find the total of 69.21, 34.69 and 83.85.

☐

21 Round each number to the nearest 50.

41 873 ☐   91 921 ☐   61 604 ☐

22 What is the rule for this pattern?

7.96, 7.93, 7.90, 7.87

☐

1

$$\begin{array}{r} 896\,115 \\ 90\,400 \\ +\ \ 386\,382 \\ \hline \end{array}$$

2 The length of a fully grown snake is 1800 cm. The length of a baby snake is 19 cm. What is the difference between the lengths of the two snakes?

3 Complete:

×	40 000	60 000	80 000
8			

4 True or false?

71 045 ÷ 9 = 7894

5 Ruby added together the fractions on the two cards. What was the answer?

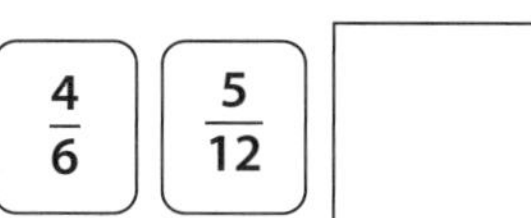

6 There were 60 ice creams in a shop. After $\frac{3}{5}$ of the ice creams were sold, how many ice creams were left?

7 Phil has 50 counters. Stuart has 35 more counters than Phil and Tilly has 17 more counters than Stuart. How many counters does Tilly have?

8 Write 3:25 am as 24-hour time.

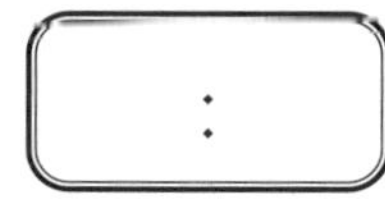

9 Declan's drawing class starts at 7:15 pm. It goes for 75 minutes. What time does the class finish?

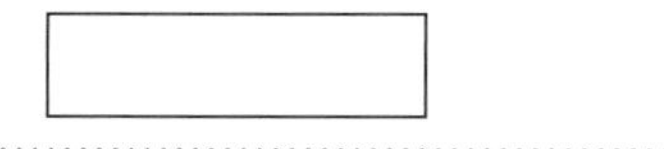

11 Which rectangle has the longer perimeter?

	Length	Width	Perimeter
A	5 m	7 m	
B	4 m	3 m	

12 Complete with >, < or =.

13 Complete the table.

Number of hexagons	1	2	3	4
Number of sides				

14 Draw the top view of:

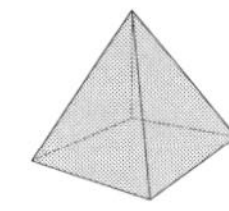

15 Continue the pattern.

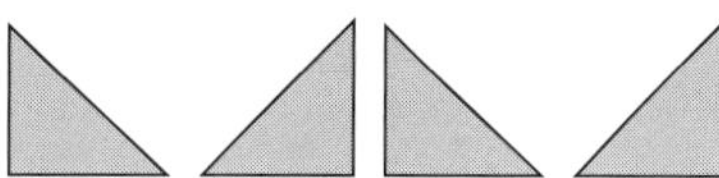

16 Draw and label the two points on the coordinate axes.
A (−3, −1)
B (5, 0)

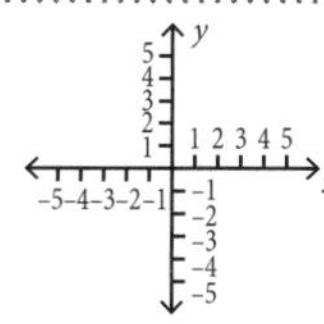

17 What is the value of *a*?

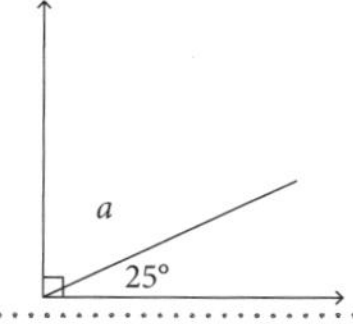

18 Bridget has a $\frac{5}{10}$ chance of **not** selecting a black card. What is this as a percentage?

19 What is the chance (as a percentage) of getting 2 heads when flipping 2 coins?

20 How many people have cash and a credit card?

	Have a credit card	Don't have a credit card
Have cash	22	12
Don't have cash	64	3

21 What fraction of the circle has the numbers 4 or 8?

22 What fraction of the circle has the number 1?

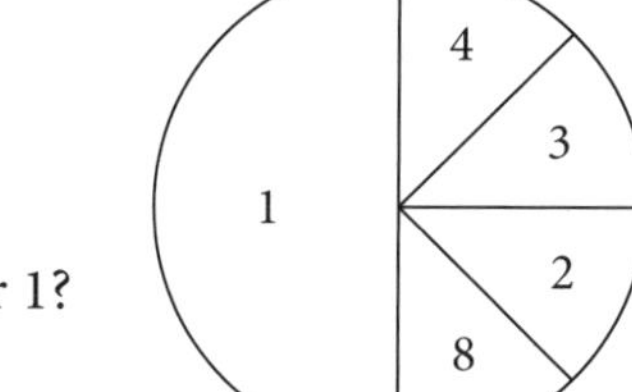

1

+	11	35	8	49	52	26
60						

2

−	96	71	56	82	65	100
50						

3

×	5	4	9	1	11	7
4						

4

×	2	10	8	12	6	3
10						

5

÷	6	30	72	18	66	36
6						

6

÷	27	18	63	81	45	90
9						

7 Estimate by first rounding each number to the nearest hundred.

$7895 + 91\,472 = \square$

8 What is the total length?

632 cm + 781 cm + 948 cm = ☐

9

$$\begin{array}{r} 217\,683 \text{ tonnes} \\ -\ 119\,482 \text{ tonnes} \\ \hline \end{array}$$

10 What is the difference between $8530 and $2960?

☐

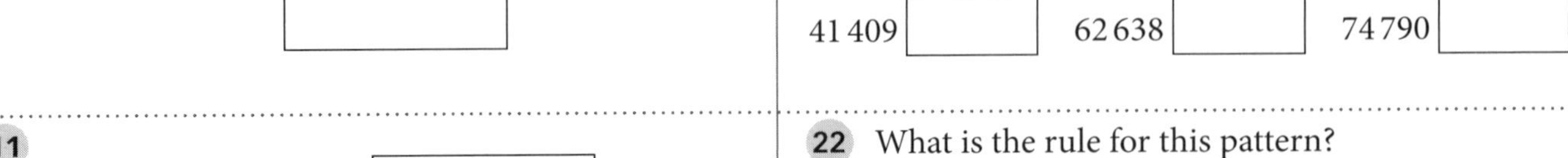

11

10 × 110 = ☐

10 × 1100 = ☐

12 Complete the boxes.

$6 \times 5 = \square = 3 \times \square$

13

450 ÷ 5 = ☐

720 ÷ 9 = ☐

14 How much would 8 athletes receive if they shared 30 apples equally?

☐

15 Circle the smallest number.

109 000 117 000 403 000 208 000

16 What is 5 °C less than the temperature shown? ☐

17 Round each of the following to the nearest 5c.

$413.56 ☐ $29.72 ☐ $821.39 ☐

18 Find 10% of $15.00.

☐

19 Riley measured the weight of 8 bags of apples. Each bag weighs 2.95 kg. What is the total weight of the apples altogether?

☐

20 Find the total of 66.73, 911.05 and 817.64.

☐

21 Round each number to the nearest 50.

41 409 ☐ 62 638 ☐ 74 790 ☐

22 What is the rule for this pattern?

11.04, 11.07, 11.10, 11.13

☐

1

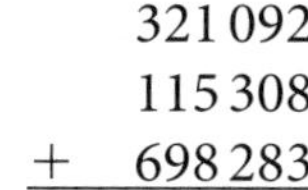

2 A baby kangaroo weighs 2 g. An adult kangaroo weighs 80 000 g. What is the difference between the weights of the two kangaroos?

3 Complete:

×	60 000	20 000	30 000
9			

4 True or false?

38 538 ÷ 6 = 6423

5 James added together the fractions on the three cards. What was the answer?

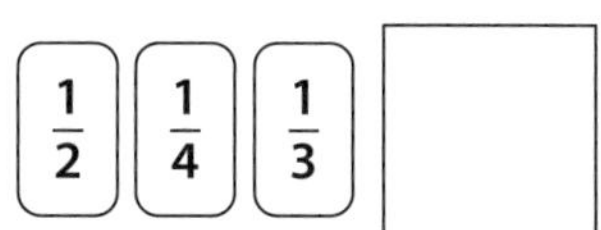

6 There are 84 students in Year 6 and $\frac{3}{7}$ of them walk to school. How many students walk to school?

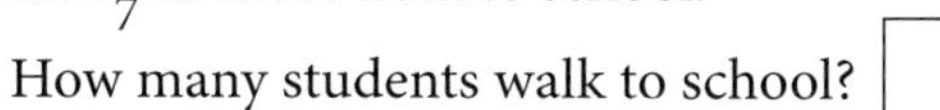

7 There are 30 textas in each of 4 packets and there are 20 textas in each of 7 packets. How many textas are there altogether?

8 Write 1:05 am as 24-hour time.

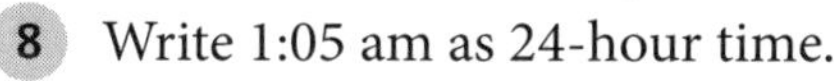

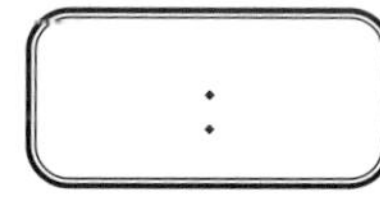

9 Lily's singing class starts at 7:40 pm. It goes for 50 minutes. What time does the class finish?

10

9400 mL = ☐ L

11 Which rectangle has the longer perimeter?

	Length	Width	Perimeter
A	7 m	9 m	
B	8 m	6 m	

12 Complete with >, < or =.

13 Complete the table.

Number of octagons	1	2	3	4
Number of sides				

14 Draw the top view of:

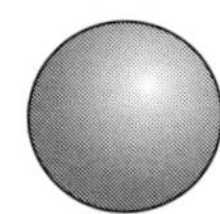

15 Continue the pattern.

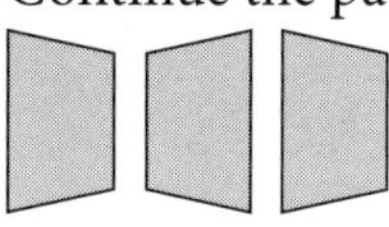

16 Draw and label the two points on the coordinate axes.
A (−4, −3)
B (−2, 1)

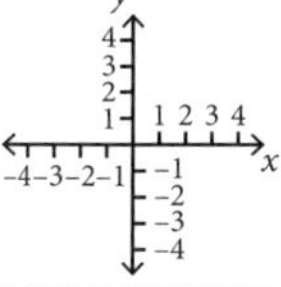

17 What is the value of *a*?

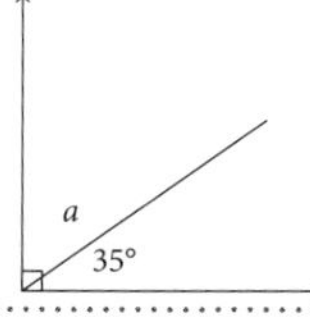

18 Rob has a $\frac{4}{10}$ chance of selecting a pink card. What is this as a percentage?

19 What is the chance of getting a tail and a head (in any order) when flipping 2 coins?

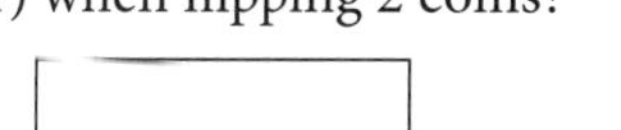

20 How many people go interstate and overseas?

	Going overseas	Not going overseas
Going interstate	6	24
Not going interstate	4	35

21 What fraction of students play netball?

22 Which is the least popular activity?

1

+	36	47	92	57	79	63
79						

2

–	100	96	114	72	63	85
36						

3

×	1	9	5	8	11	3
2						

4

×	4	7	2	6	12	10
11						

5

÷	70	100	30	10	60	90
10						

6

÷	48	36	72	96	60	144
12						

7

$$\begin{array}{r} \$46\,275 \\ + \quad \$12\,386 \\ \hline \end{array} \qquad \begin{array}{r} \$32\,110 \\ + \ \$26\,473 \\ \hline \end{array}$$

8

$$\begin{array}{r} 462\,381 \\ 942\,117 \\ +\ 149\,805 \\ \hline \end{array}$$

9 Subtract $720 from $9000.

10 Fill in the missing boxes.

$$\begin{array}{rrrr} 8 & \square & 7 & 0 \\ - & 7 & \square & 3 \\ \hline \square & 8 & 4 & \square \end{array}$$

11

10 × 14 = ☐

20 × 14 = ☐

30 × 14 = ☐

12 If there are 20 lots of 40 books, what is the total number of books?

13 How many groups of 3 are in 421?

14 429 eggs are placed into cartons of 6. How many cartons are needed?

15 Label +6 on the number line.

–10 0 10

16 How many thousands are in 132 468?

17 Find 25% of $20.

18 What is the difference between $43.85 and $99.72?

19 Find 9.2 ÷ 4.

20 There are 10 pieces of pipe. Each piece of pipe is 3.2 m long. What is the total length of all of the pipe?

21 Round each number to the nearest hundred.

432 485 ☐ 869 108 ☐

22 Find the missing numbers.

200 + ☐ = 560

900 – ☐ = 250

1

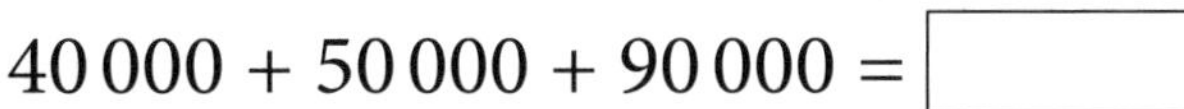

2 What is the difference between 90 000 and 48 691?

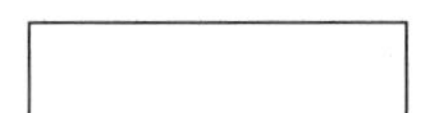

3 In the warehouse, there are 2040 packets of tennis balls. There are 6 tennis balls in each packet. How many tennis balls are there altogether?

4

46 291 ÷ 8 =

5 Write each of the decimals as a fraction.

A 0.6 **B** 0.91 **C** 0.03

6 Zander has 2 cakes. He gives $\frac{3}{4}$ of one cake to his classmates. He gives $\frac{1}{2}$ of the other cake to his family. How much cake does Zander have left altogether?

7

4 × ☐ = 48

48 ÷ ☐ = 4

8 Draw 21:50 on the clockface.

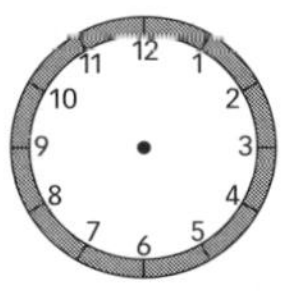

9 Kylie's soccer training starts in half an hour. At what time does her soccer training start?

10 Circle the shortest length.

42 cm 400 mm 0.45 m

11 Which shape has the greatest area?

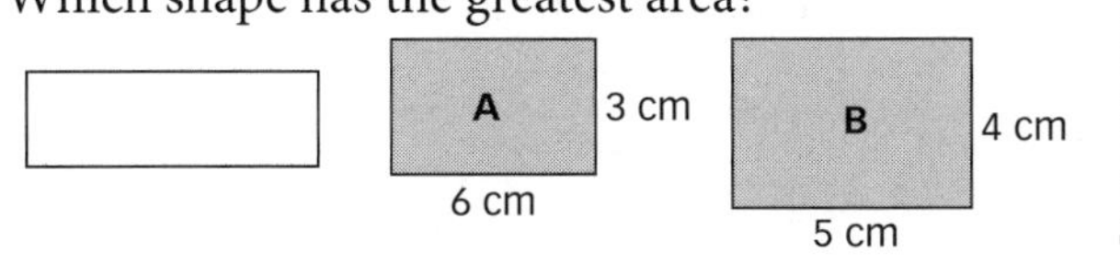

12 What is the total mass?

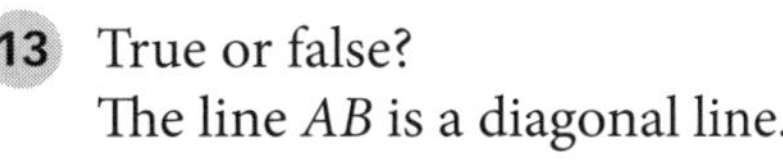

13 True or false?
The line AB is a diagonal line.

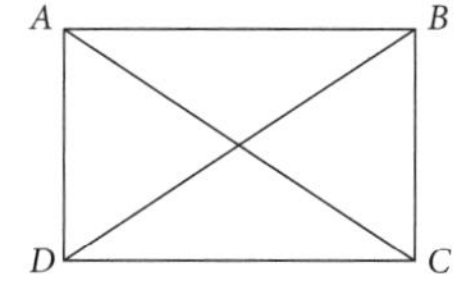

14 List all the different shapes of the faces of a cube.

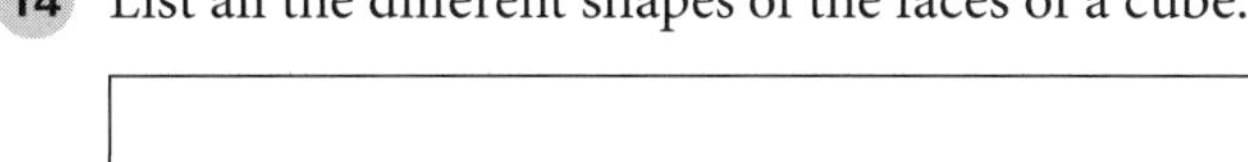

15 Is this pattern based on reflection, translation or rotation?

16 Draw the reflection of the shape.

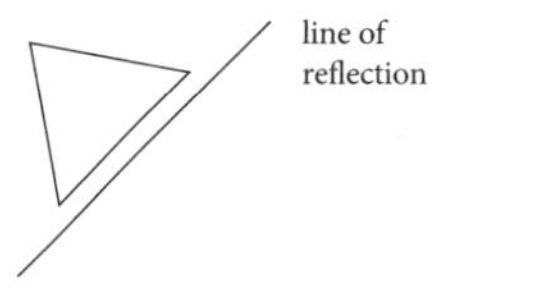

17 Find the value of a.

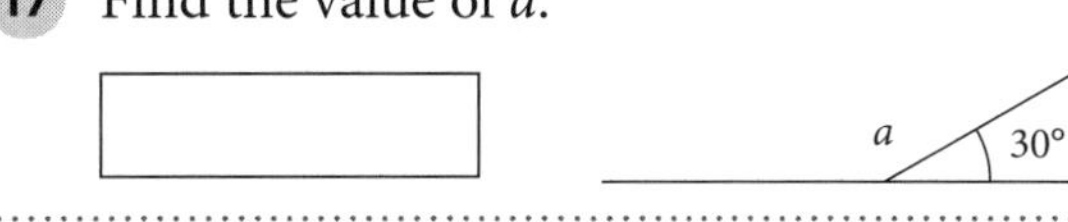

Eliza conducted a survey of 50 people to find their favourite drink.

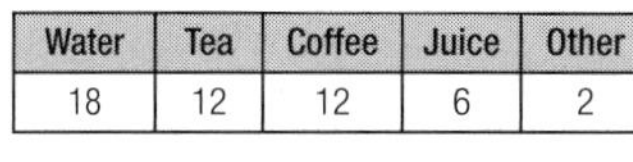

Water	Tea	Coffee	Juice	Other
18	12	12	6	2

18 Use the table to predict how many people in each 100 would prefer coffee.

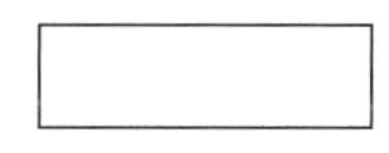

19 Use the table to predict how many people in each 1000 would prefer water.

20 Create a table for the following set of data:

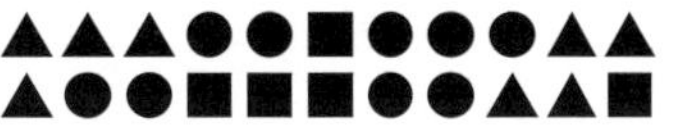

21 How many more people prefer chocolate ice cream to vanilla?

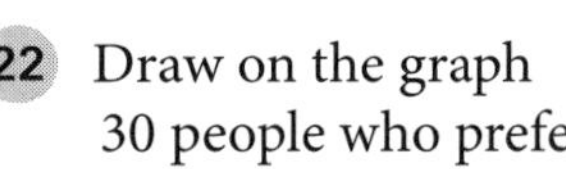

22 Draw on the graph 30 people who prefer caramel ice cream.

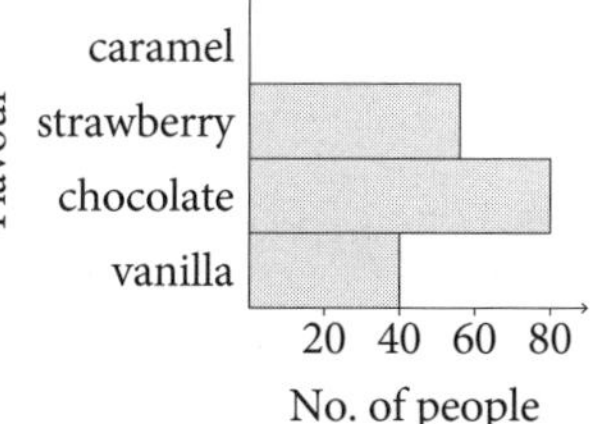

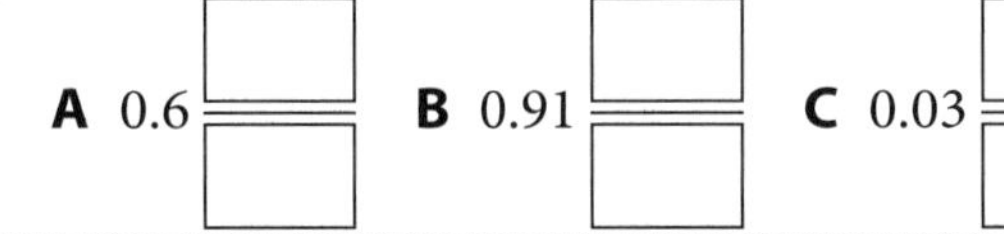

1

+	37	71	16	86	93	48
69						

2

−	90	49	60	96	71	87
47						

3

×	7	3	10	2	12	8
2						

4

×	1	11	5	9	4	6
11						

5

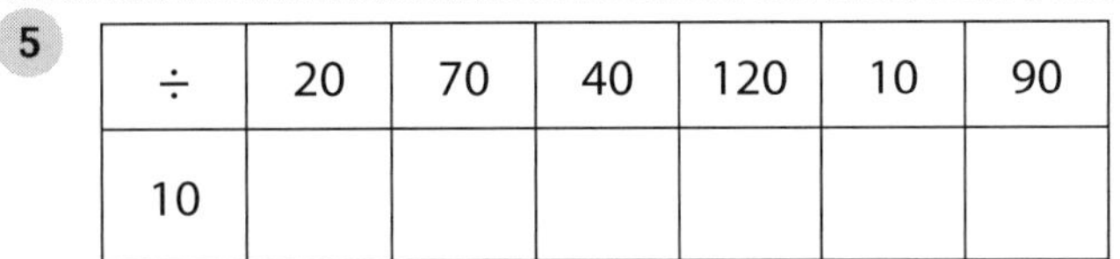

÷	20	70	40	120	10	90
10						

6

÷	120	12	108	84	36	144
12						

7

$$\begin{array}{r} \$119\,385 \\ +\ \$247\,119 \\ \hline \end{array} \qquad \begin{array}{r} \$85\,024 \\ +\ \$79\,385 \\ \hline \end{array}$$

8

$$\begin{array}{r} 432\,105 \\ 117\,195 \\ +\ 468\,387 \\ \hline \end{array}$$

9 What is \$2000 take away \$250?

10 Fill in the missing boxes.

$$\begin{array}{r} 8\ \square\ 0\ \square \\ -\ \square\ 9\ \square\ 6 \\ \hline 1\ 1\ 9\ 4 \end{array}$$

11

10 × 75 =

20 × 75 =

30 × 75 =

12 If there are 30 boxes of 60 bottles of water, what is the total number of bottles?

13 How many groups of 6 are in 851?

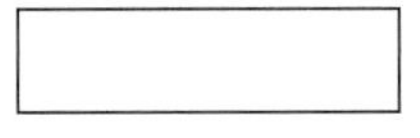

14 320 bread rolls are packed into bags of 6. How many bags are needed?

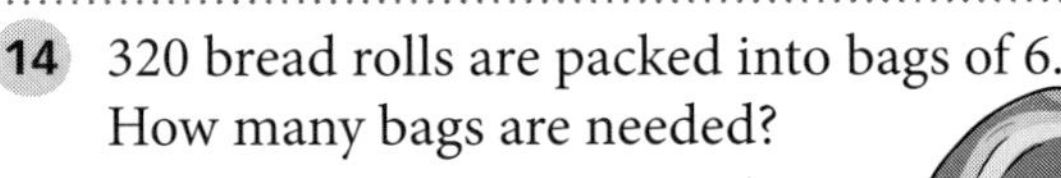

15 Label −8 on the number line.

−10 0 10

16 How many thousands are in 261 483?

17 Find 25% of \$32.

18 What is the difference between \$621.63 and \$319.87?

19 Find 7.32 ÷ 6.

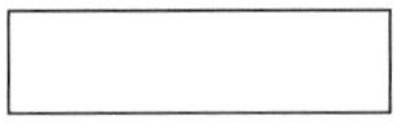

20 There are 10 bottles of juice. Each bottle has 1.25 L of juice. What is the total volume of juice?

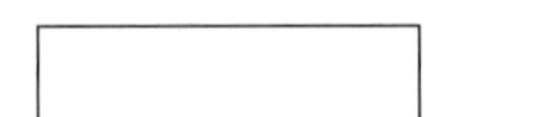

21 Round each number to the nearest hundred.

610 639 621 098

22 Find the missing numbers.

160 + □ = 530

920 − □ = 790

1

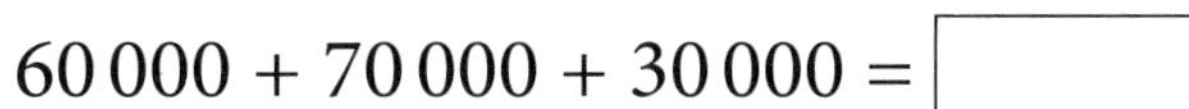

$60\,000 + 70\,000 + 30\,000 =$ ☐

2 What is the difference between 80 000 and 79 864?

3 In the warehouse, there are 4980 packets of socks. There are 4 socks in each packet. How many socks are there altogether?

4

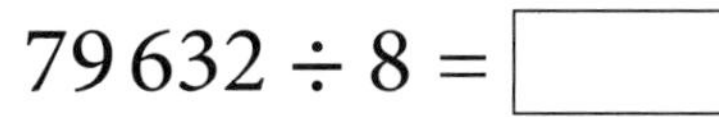

$79\,632 \div 8 =$ ☐

5 Write each of the decimals as a fraction.

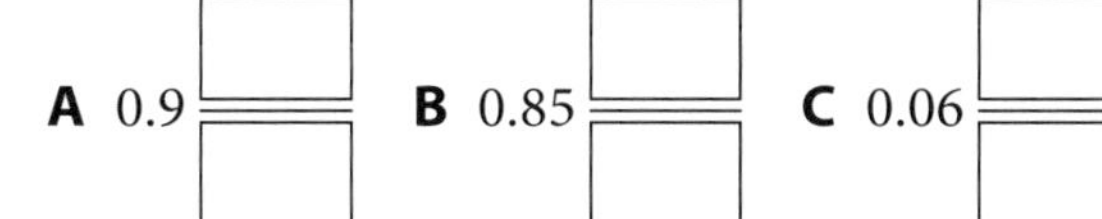

A 0.9 **B** 0.85 **C** 0.06

6 Andrew has 2 bags of treats. He gives $\frac{1}{3}$ of one bag to his brother. He gives $\frac{5}{6}$ of the other bag to his friends. How much does Andrew have left of the bags altogether?

7

$12 \times$ ☐ $= 84$

$84 \div$ ☐ $= 12$

8 Draw 21:10 on the clockface.

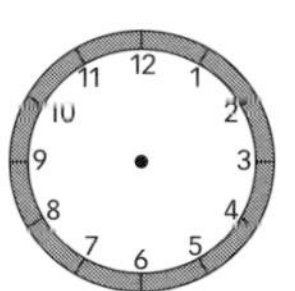

9 Tom's tennis lesson starts in 40 minutes. What time does his tennis lesson start?

10 Circle the smallest mass.

9.1 kg 9500 g 9.613 kg

11 Which shape has the greatest area?

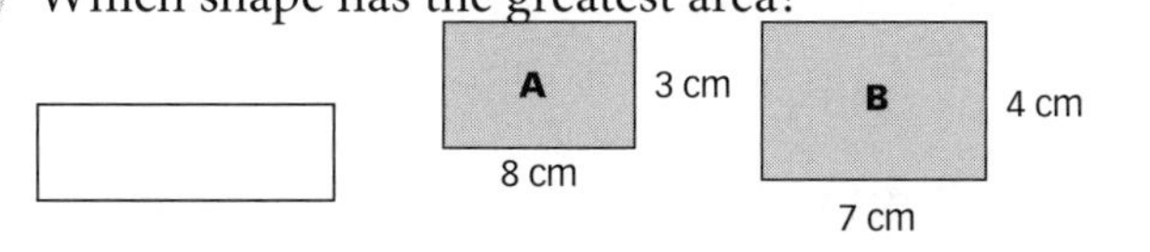

12 What is the total volume?

2 mL + 0.5 L + 2 L = ☐

13 True or false? The lines *AB* and *DC* are parallel.

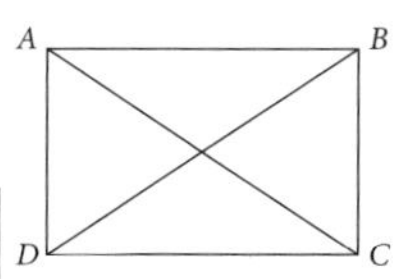

14 List all the different shapes of the faces of a triangular-based pyramid.

15 Is this pattern based on reflection, translation or rotation?

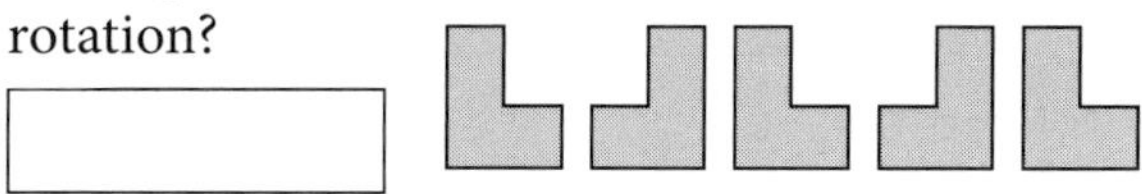

16 Draw the reflection of the shape.

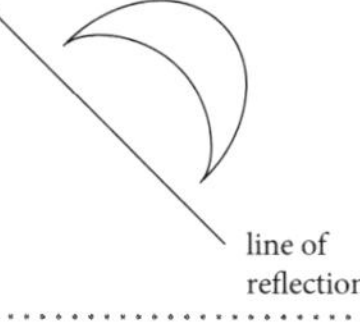

17 Find the value of *a*.

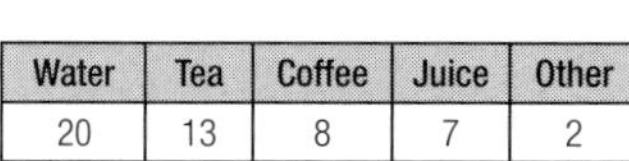

Erik conducted a survey of 50 people to find their favourite drink.

Water	Tea	Coffee	Juice	Other
20	13	8	7	2

18 Use the table to predict how many people in each 100 would prefer tea.

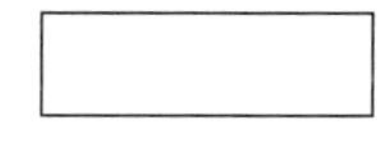

19 Use the table to predict how many people in each 1000 would prefer water.

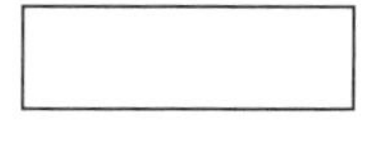

20 Create a table for the following set of data.

21 How many more students are enrolled in Science than Maths?

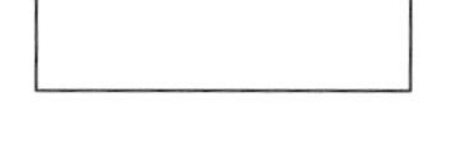

22 Draw on the graph 75 students who are enrolled in Geography.

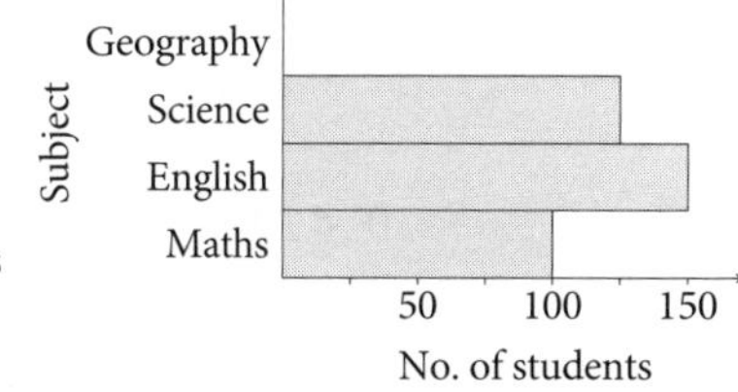

UNIT 23A

1

+	67	83	110	43	90	71
75						

2

−	100	79	94	114	81	60
53						

3

×	6	0	9	3	10	4
2						

4

×	2	8	5	11	7	1
11						

5

÷	110	10	70	30	40	90
10						

6

÷	144	72	36	60	12	132
12						

7

$92 114
+ $35 846

$110 427
+ $320 085

8

805 216
117 408
+ 249 461

9 Take $710 from $3000.

10 Fill in the missing boxes.

8 5 ☐ 3
− ☐ 4 0 ☐
6 ☐ 5 5

11

10 × 33 = ☐

20 × 33 = ☐

30 × 33 = ☐

12 What is the total number of students if there are 40 groups of 20 students?

13 How many groups of 5 are in 725?

14 600 marbles are put equally into 8 boxes. How many marbles are in each box?

15 Label 9 on the number line.

−10 0 10

16 How many thousands are in 30 109?

17 Find 25% of $44.

18 What is the difference between $621.80 and $712.90?

19 Find 8.1 ÷ 3.

20 There are 10 balls of string. Each ball has 4.2 m of string. What is the total length of all of the string?

21 Round each number to the nearest hundred.

439 605 ☐ 711 402 ☐

22 Find the missing numbers.

240 + ☐ = 830

910 − ☐ = 470

1

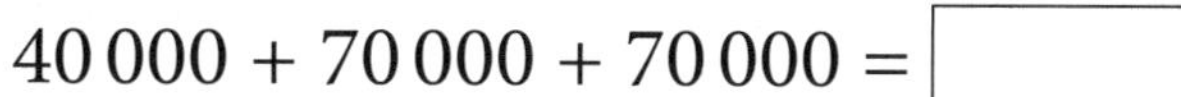

$40\,000 + 70\,000 + 70\,000 =$ ☐

2 What is the difference between 300 000 and 295 106?

3 In the warehouse, there are 1176 packets of pencils. There are 12 pencils in each packet. How many pencils are there altogether? ☐

4

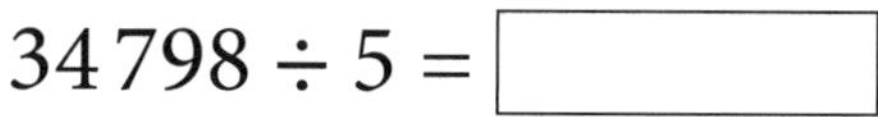

$34\,798 \div 5 =$ ☐

5 Write each of the decimals as a fraction.

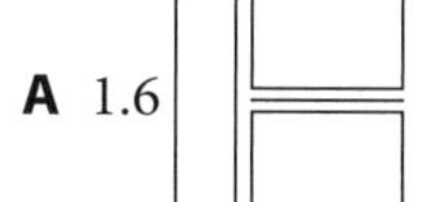

A 1.6 ☐ $\frac{☐}{☐}$ **B** 0.03 $\frac{☐}{☐}$ **C** 0.45 $\frac{☐}{☐}$

6 Robyn has sheep on her farm. She put $\frac{3}{10}$ of the sheep in one paddock and $\frac{2}{5}$ of the sheep in a second paddock. What fraction of the sheep does Robyn put in the last paddock? ☐

7

$7 \times$ ☐ $= 77$

$77 \div$ ☐ $= 11$

8 Draw 14:25 on the clockface.

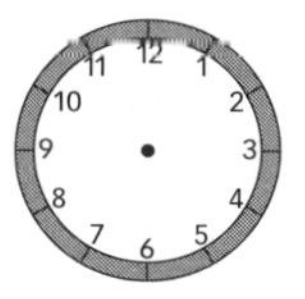

9 Tanya's basketball training starts in three-quarters of an hour. At what time does her basketball training start? ☐

10 Circle the smallest volume.

31 mL   3 L   4000 mL

11 Which shape has the greatest area? ☐

A: 10 m × 3 m   B: 6 m × 6 m

12 What is the total mass?

0.9 kg + 400 g + 3000 g = ☐

13 True or false? The line *DC* is horizontal. ☐

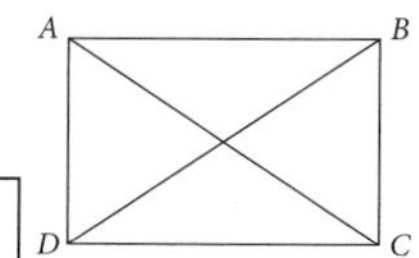

14 List all the different shapes of the faces of a triangular prism.

☐

15 Is this pattern based on reflection, translation or rotation? ☐

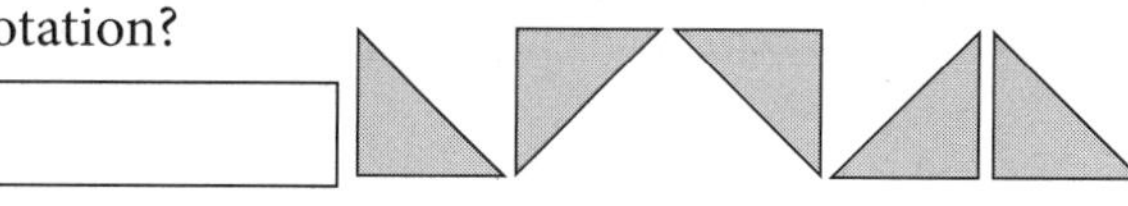

16 Draw the reflection of the shape.

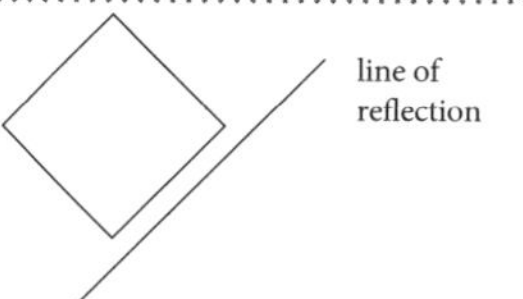

17 Find the value of *a*. ☐

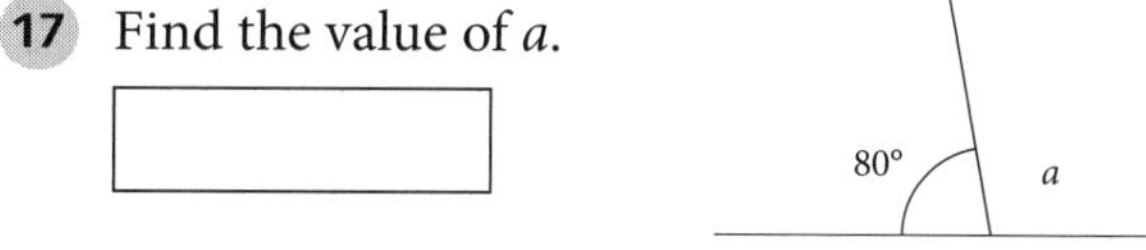

Toby conducted a survey of 50 people to find their favourite sport.

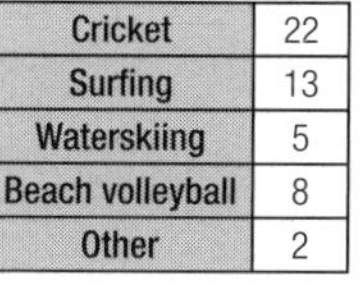

Cricket	22
Surfing	13
Waterskiing	5
Beach volleyball	8
Other	2

18 Use the table to predict how many people in each 100 would prefer waterskiing. ☐

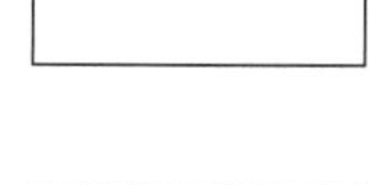

19 Use the table to predict how many people in each 1000 would prefer surfing. ☐

20 Create a table for the following set of data.

21 How many more pencils than pens are there? ☐

22 Draw 350 crayons on the graph.

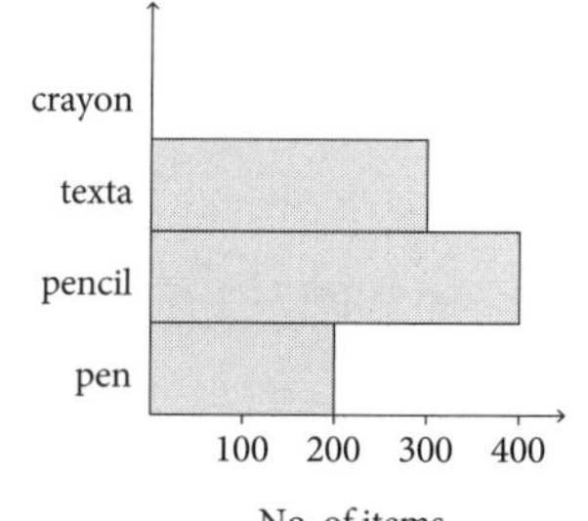

1

+	35	61	57	43	29	10
40						

2

–	31	72	56	99	45	101
20						

3

×	2	11	5	8	9	3
4						

4

×	6	1	10	7	12	4
11						

5

÷	60	6	36	54	18	72
6						

6

÷	63	54	81	72	27	108
9						

7

$11 638
+ $29 403

8 46 km + 927 km + 319 km = ☐

9

38 561 cm
– 21 763 cm

10

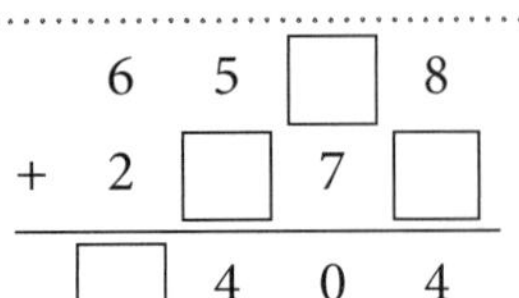

11 Complete the pattern.

4 × 30 = ☐

4 × 300 = ☐

4 × 3000 = ☐

12 What are the missing numbers?

12 × ☐ = ☐ = 6 × 8

13 560 ÷ 8 =

A 7 **B** 70
C 80 **D** 800

14 432 apples are placed into bags of 8. How many bags are needed?

☐

15 Which is the smallest number?

A 120 000 **B** 460 000
C 390 000 **D** 106 000

16 Which is a composite number?

A 23 **B** 41
C 52 **C** 67

17 What is 25% of $12?

☐

18 What is $3.26 rounded to the nearest 5c?

A $3.30 **B** $3.25
C $3.50 **D** $3.00

19 Cathy has 5 pieces of string. Each piece is 4.80 m long. What is the total length of the string?

☐

20 8.96 ÷ 4 =

21 Round 149 863 to the nearest hundred.

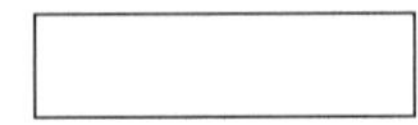

22 What is the missing number?

480 + ☐ = 1070

1 80 000 + 40 000 + 90 000 =

2 What is the difference in height between a 5500-mm adult giraffe and a 1800-mm baby giraffe? ______ mm

3 In a market there are 9 crates of apricots. Each crate has 1500 apricots. How many apricots are there altogether?

4 True or false?

$$3864 \div 4 = 966$$

5 What is 0.05 written as a fraction?

A $\frac{1}{5}$ **B** $\frac{5}{10}$

C $\frac{5}{100}$ **D** $\frac{1}{2}$

$$1 - \frac{3}{5} =$$

$$8 \times \square = 72$$

8 Draw 18:50 on the clockface.

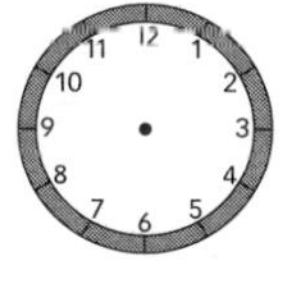

9 Ben's dance class starts in 40 minutes. At what time does his dance class start?

10 9600 mL =

A 9 L **B** 9.6 L

C 96 L **D** 960 L

11 Which rectangle has the greatest area?

	Length (cm)	Width (cm)
A	5	4
B	3	8
C	11	2
D	7	3

12 Complete with <, > or =.

1.9 kg ☐ 2000 g

13 Which line is parallel to DC?

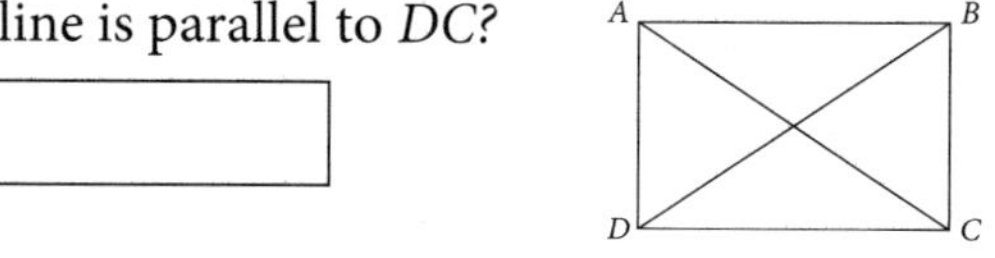

14 Tick all of the shapes of the faces of a triangular prism.

A triangle **B** rectangle

C square **D** parallelogram

15 Is this pattern a

A reflection?

B rotation?

C translation?

16 Draw and label the two points on the coordinate axes.

A (3, 0) **B** (0, −2)

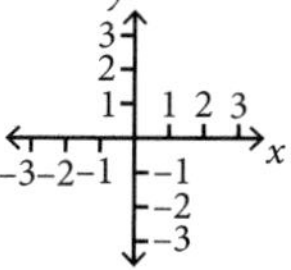

17 What is the value of a?

a
35°

18 Phillip has a $\frac{1}{10}$ chance of selecting a red ball from a bag. What is this as a percentage?

19 Alice conducted a survey of 50 people to find their favourite drink. Use the information to predict how many people in each 100 would prefer coffee.

Water	15
Tea	13
Coffee	13
Juice	7
Other	2

20 Here is a two-way table. How many people don't like music but do like sport?

	Likes sport	Doesn't like sport
Likes music	15	5
Doesn't like music	4	6

21 What fraction of people selected green?

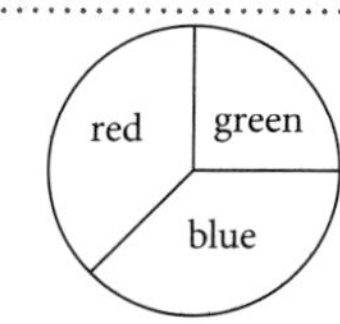

22 The graph shows the preferred breakfast items for a group of people. What was the most popular breakfast item?

Breakfast
mushrooms
bacon
eggs
spinach
5 10 15 20 25
No. of people

1 Dylan has \$42 398 in one bank account and \$31 660 in a second bank account. How much money does Dylan have altogether?

A \$73 958
B \$74 058
C \$74 068
D \$74 958

2 In one week Holly ran 14 km, 21 km and 36 km.

How far did Holly run? ☐ km

3 What is the difference in length between 39 621 cm and 47 950 cm?

A 8329 cm
B 87 571 cm
C 12 329 cm
D 12 331 cm

4 What is the missing number?

$\square \times 5 = 15$

$\square \times 50 = 150$

$\square \times 500 = 1500$

A 3
B 5
C 10
D 15

5 693 bananas are divided into bags of 9 bananas.

How many bags are needed? ☐

6 Which is a prime number?

A 9
B 31
C 42
D 56

7 The price of the board game has 25% off.
How much is the game reduced by?

A $4
B $6
C $8
D $9

8 The total cost of the shopping was $426.13. What is this rounded to the nearest 5c?

A $426.00
B $426.10
C $426.15
D $427.00

9 Each bag of apples weighed 3.90 kg. Gail bought 5 bags. What was the total weight of the apples?

 kg

10 What is the missing number?

$$30 \times \square = 240$$

A 40
B 6
C 8
D 80

11 What is 10 000 – 4698?

A 5302
B 5402
C 6412
D 14 698

12 What is 0.2 written as a fraction?

A $\frac{1}{2}$
B $\frac{2}{10}$
C $\frac{2}{5}$
D $\frac{2}{100}$

13 Amelia's singing class starts in 45 minutes. The time now is shown on the clock.
What time does the singing class start?

A 5:35
B 5:25
C 4:45
D 5:05

14 Joe wanted to relabel a container from 4700 mL to litres. Which label is correct?

A 4 L
B 4.7 L
C 47 L
D 470 L

15 Which rectangle has the longest perimeter?

	Length (cm)	Width (cm)
A	5	4
B	3	8
C	7	3
D	6	4

16 Which line is diagonal?

A *AB*
B *BD*
C *CD*
D *DA*

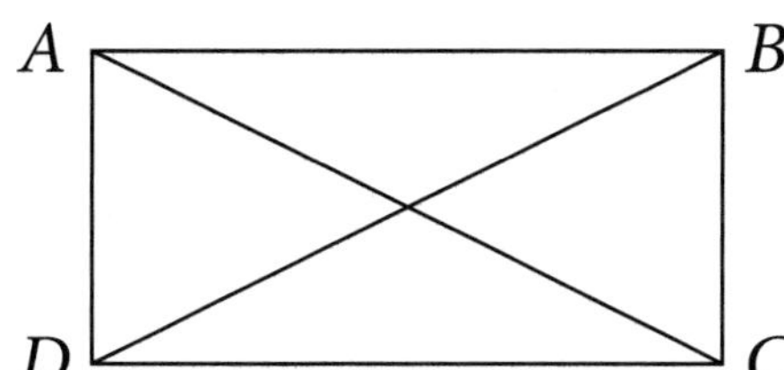

17 Erin finds the value of a. What is that value?

A 30°
B 60°
C 120°
D 150°

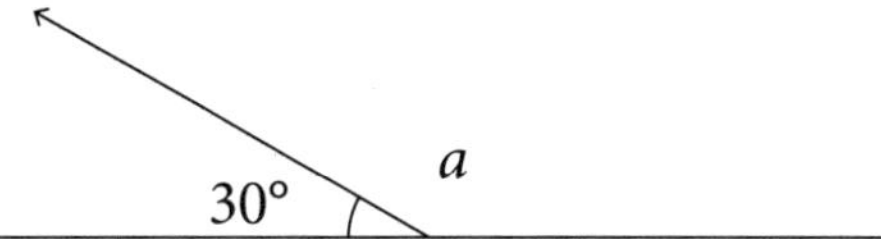

18 Henry has a $\frac{3}{10}$ chance of selecting a blue card from a pack of cards. This is a

A 3% chance.
B 30% chance.
C 13% chance.
D 7% chance.

19 Here is information collected about whether some children have skateboards or scooters. How many children have a scooter but **not** a skateboard?

A 15
B 6
C 9
D 10

	Has a skateboard	Doesn't have a skateboard
Has a scooter	15	6
Doesn't have a scooter	9	10

20 What is the least used shape in the maths book?

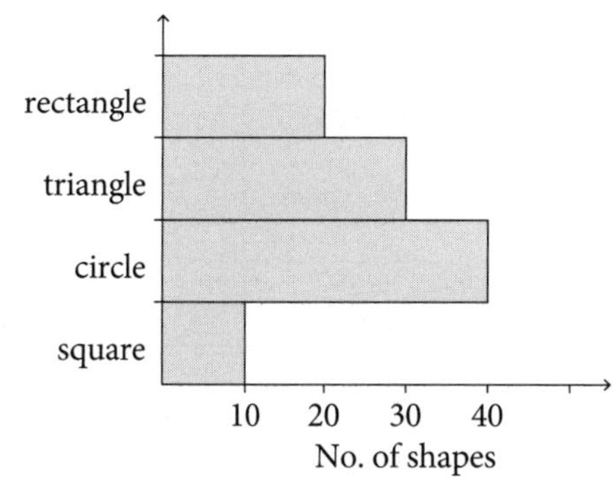

1

+	64	79	33	47	59	85
53						

2

−	110	93	71	82	60	52
48						

3

×	1	6	7	4	12	9
2						

4

×	5	8	2	10	11	3
11						

5

÷	100	40	20	30	70	10
10						

6

÷	132	12	60	36	72	120
12						

7

$10 936
+ $42 118

$426 831
+ $357 798

8

743 825
972 106
+ 384 117

9 Find $8700 less than $40 000.

☐

10 Fill in the missing boxes.

  5 1 1 8
− 4 ☐ 1 ☐
  3 ☐ 4

11

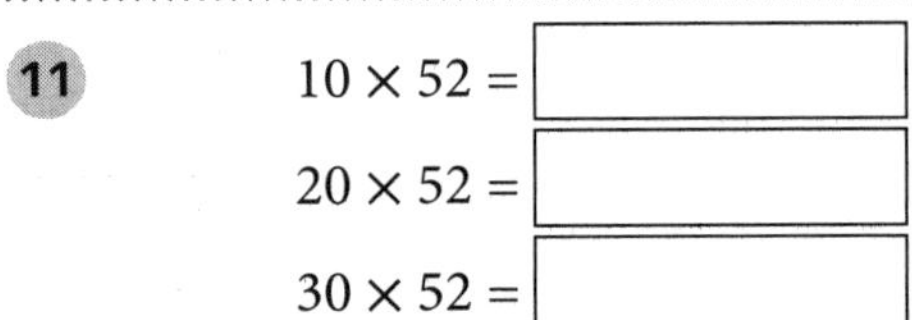

10 × 52 = ☐

20 × 52 = ☐

30 × 52 = ☐

12 What is the total number of biscuits in 30 packets of 20 biscuits?

☐

13 Find how many groups of 6 in 621?

☐

14 If 318 sushi rolls are divided into boxes of 4, how many boxes are needed?

☐

15 Label 0 on the number line.

−10 0 10

16 How many thousands are in 129 117?

☐

17 Find 25% of $36.

☐

18 What is the difference between $641.72 and $719.25?

☐

19 Find 7.6 ÷ 4.

☐

20 There are 10 bags of cherries. Each bag weighs 1.75 kg. What is the total weight of all the cherries?

☐

21 Round each number to the nearest hundred.

496 305 ☐ 791 149 ☐

22 Find the missing numbers.

630 + ☐ = 910

850 − ☐ = 170

1 $90\,000 + 60\,000 + 40\,000 =$ ☐

2 What is the difference between 200 000 and 140 007?

3 In the warehouse, there are 1209 packets of wrapping paper. There are 8 sheets of wrapping paper in each packet. How many pieces of wrapping paper are there altogether?

4 $42\,831 \div 9 =$ ☐

5 Write each of the decimals as a fraction.

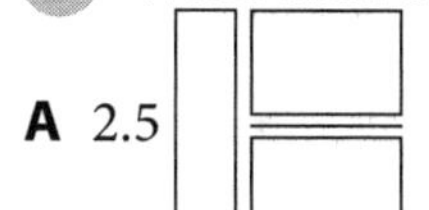
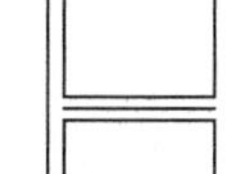
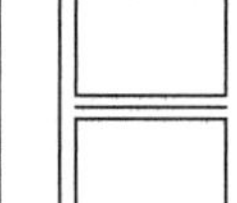

A 2.5 **B** 1.06 **C** 1.91

6 Sam had a length of wood. She used $\frac{1}{2}$ of it to fix a wall. She used half of the remaining piece to make a shelf. What fraction of the original piece of wood did Sam have left?

7 $7 \times$ ☐ $= 63$

$63 \div$ ☐ $= 7$

8 Draw 20:40 on the clockface.

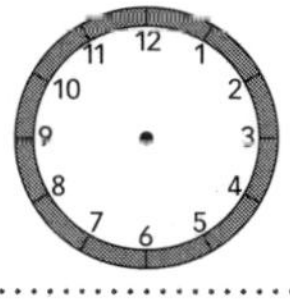

9 Alex's music class starts in 50 minutes. At what time does his music class start?

10 Circle the shortest length.

400 m 0.45 km 46 000 cm

11 Which shape has the greatest area?

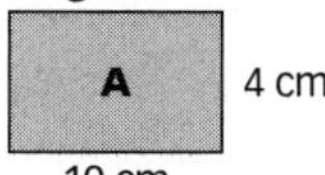

12 What is the total volume?

0.6 L + 6000 mL + 1.3 L = ☐

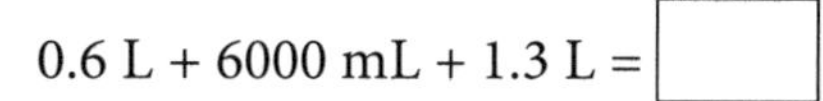

13 True or false?
The line *BD* is vertical.

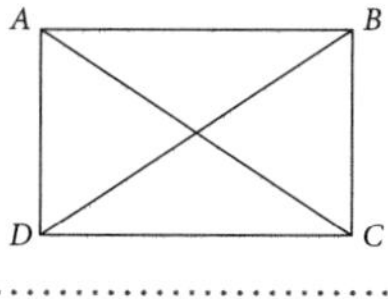

14 List all the different shapes of the faces of a cylinder.

15 Is this pattern based on reflection, translation or rotation?

16 Draw the reflection of the shape.

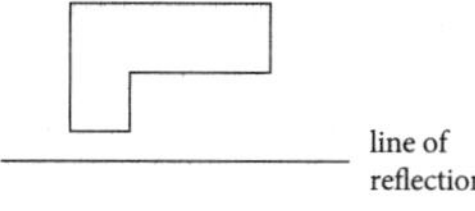

17 Find the value of *a*.

Jess conducted a survey of 50 people to find their favourite colour.

Colour	Number
Red	10
Blue	12
Yellow	8
Green	14
Purple	6

18 Use the table to predict how many people in each 100 would prefer yellow.

19 Use the table to predict how many people in each 1000 would prefer blue.

20 Create a table for the following set of data.

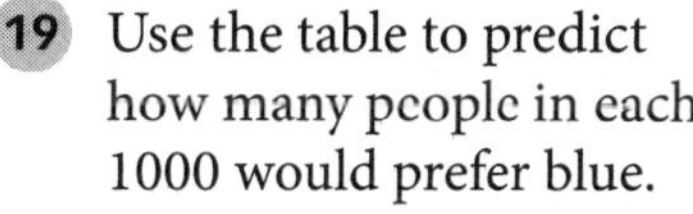

21 How many more spoons than forks are there?

22 Draw 90 serving utensils on the graph.

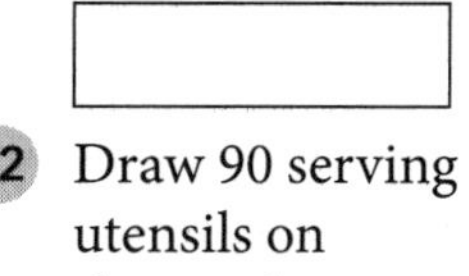

UNIT 25A

1

+	69	71	93	47	52	104
47						

2

–	120	81	68	93	105	72
59						

3

×	6	2	8	4	9	12
2						

4

×	1	10	3	5	11	7
11						

5

÷	90	10	60	30	80	40
10						

6

÷	120	72	24	96	48	144
12						

7

$114 325
+ $119 472

$85 762
+ $93 115

8

791 428
305 114
+ 405 201

9 Subtract $2100 from $40 000.

10 Fill in the missing boxes.

```
  5 1 □ 9
– 3 □ 2 7
  □ 0 3 □
```

11

10 × 87 = □

20 × 87 = □

30 × 87 = □

12 How many cans are in 70 crates of 30 drink cans?

13 How many groups of 5 are in 228?

14 Tennis balls are placed into tubes of 3 balls. How many tubes are needed for 501 tennis balls?

15 Label –1 on the number line.

–10 0 10

16 How many thousands are in 183 761?

17 Find 25% of $84.

18 What is the difference between $219.85 and $453.06?

19 Find 8.4 ÷ 6.

20 There are 10 floors in a building. Each floor is 3.1 m high. What is the total height of all the floors?

21 Round each number to the nearest hundred.

183 107 □ 798 460 □

22 Find the missing numbers.

830 + □ = 1020

470 – □ = 180

1 $70\,000 + 40\,000 + 80\,000 = \square$

2 What is the difference between 200 000 and 109 684?

3 In the warehouse, there are 4281 packets of batteries. There are 8 batteries in each packet. How many batteries are there altogether?

4 $63\,847 \div 7 = \square$

5 Write each of the decimals as a fraction.

A 6.3 **B** 0.05 **C** 0.8

6 Ally has 2 pies. She shares $\frac{3}{4}$ of one pie with her friends. She shares $\frac{2}{3}$ of the other pie with her family. How much pie does Ally have left altogether?

7

$8 \times \square = 48$

$48 \div \square = 8$

8 Draw 15:45 on the clockface.

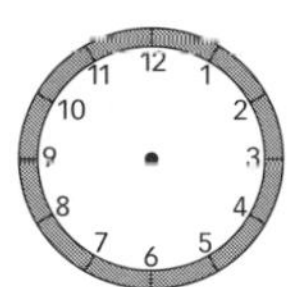

9 Hannah's singing class starts in 40 minutes. At what time does her singing class start?

10 Circle the shortest length of time.

90 s 20 min quarter of an hour

11 Which shape has the greatest area?

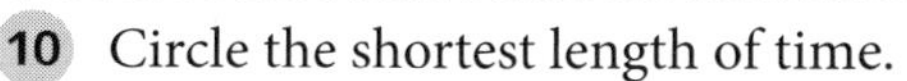

A: 8 m × 7 m B: 9 m × 6 m

12 What is the total mass?

8 kg + 400 g + 0.9 kg =

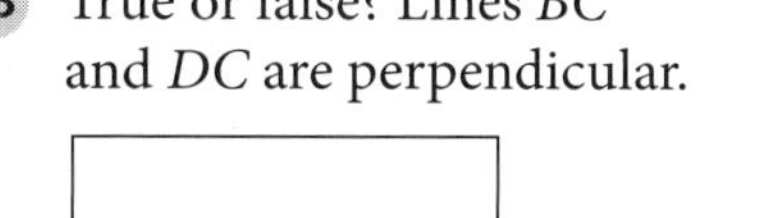

13 True or false? Lines BC and DC are perpendicular.

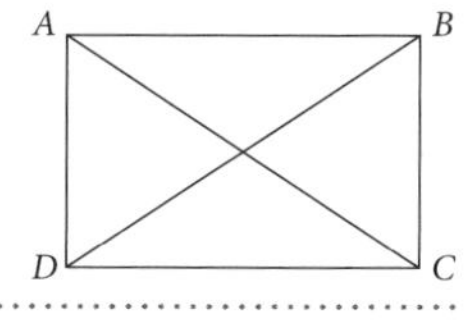

14 List all the different shapes of the faces of a square-based pyramid?

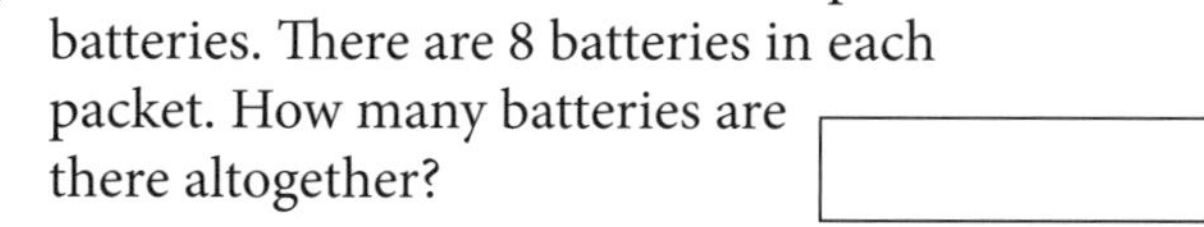

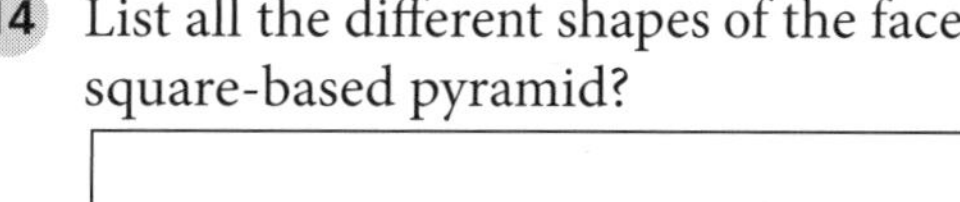

15 Is this pattern based on reflection, translation or rotation?

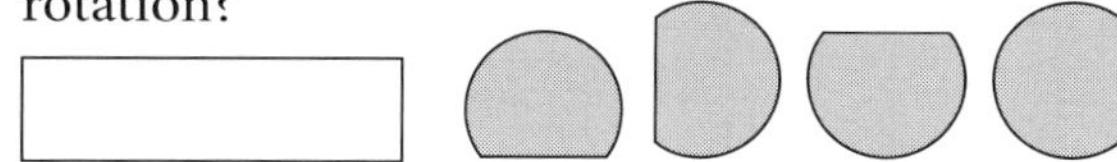

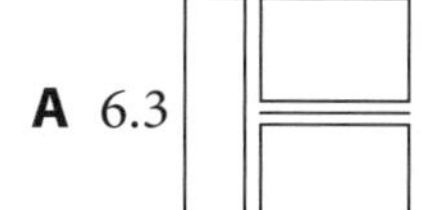

16 Draw the reflection of the shape.

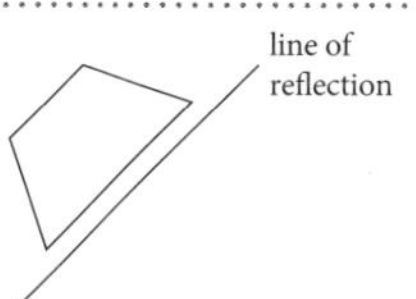

17 Find the value of a.

Joyce conducted a survey of 50 people to find their least favourite letter.

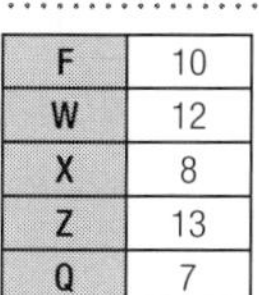

F	10
W	12
X	8
Z	13
Q	7

18 Use the table to predict how many people in each 100 would select Q.

19 Use the table to predict how many people in each 1000 would select W.

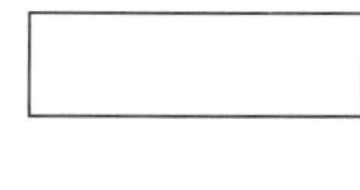

20 Create a table for the following set of data.

21 How many more bees were seen than dragonflies?

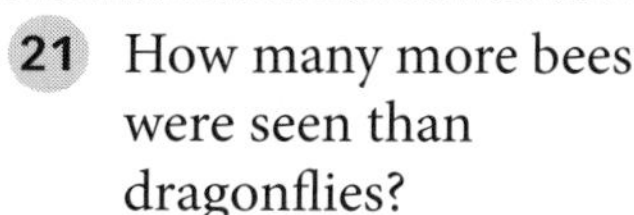

22 Draw 75 wasps on the graph.

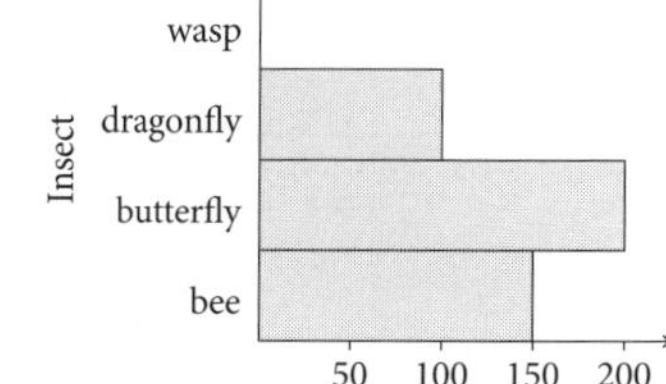

UNIT 26A

1

+	1.5	4.3	6.1	8.2	3.3	2.4
0.2						

2

−	6.1	9.3	8.4	7.6	2.7	3.5
0.1						

3

×	1	4	3	7	11	9
12						

4

×	5	2	8	10	12	6
6						

5

÷	144	12	60	48	24	120
12						

6

÷	108	18	72	45	36	99
9						

7 Find the missing numbers.

$$\begin{array}{r} 3\ 5\ \square\ 2 \\ +\ 1\ \square\ 7\ 8 \\ \hline \square\ 8\ 3\ \square \end{array}$$

8 What is the total of the 3 numbers?

3869 4158 3876

9 Find the difference between 955 630 and 10 156.

10 There were 897 mice in the barn and 268 escaped. How many mice were left in the barn?

11

$$\begin{array}{r} 521 \\ \times\ \ 6 \\ \hline \end{array}$$

12 Find the total of 8000 × 4.

13

$10\overline{)24\,680}$

14 Find the missing number.

$3\overline{)}$ 1235

15 Find the total of $2^2 + 5^2$.

16 Circle the smallest number.

427 000 378 000 109 000 423 000

17 The sunglasses have been reduced by 50%. What is the new price of the sunglasses?

Sale price:

Original price: $108

18 Round each to the nearest 5c.

$103.11 $69.72

19 Label the missing value on the number line.

7.2 7.4

20 Find 16.3 ÷ 10.

21 Round each car price to the nearest $1000.

$56 381 $85 398

22 Find the missing numbers.

$3 \times \square = 360 = \square \times 9$

UNIT 26B

1 Add the numbers on the cards together to find the total.

47 831 | 64 719 | 11 035

2 What is 32 106 less than 49 831?

3 $69\,835 \times 6 =$

4 Alexander sorted 4321 screws equally into 7 boxes. How many screws are in each box?

5 Complete the table.

Decimal	Fraction	Percentage
		90%
	$\frac{4}{10}$	
0.16		

6 Complete with <, > or =.

$\frac{4}{9}$ ☐ $\frac{2}{3}$

7 $4 \times 3 - (6 + 1) =$

8 A movie starts at 4:10. It goes for 120 minutes. At what time does the movie finish?

9 How long did the assembly go for?

9:15

Start time

End time

10 Find the total amount.

600 g 2.6 kg 3 kg

11 Find the area and perimeter of the shape.

A =

P =

13 m

5 m

12 m

12 There are 6 cubes in the base layer of a rectangular prism. If there are 3 layers in the prism, what is the volume of the rectangular prism? ☐ cm^3

13 What three-dimensional shape does this net form?

14 Draw the front view of the shape.

side

15 Rotate ☐ $\frac{1}{4}$ turn clockwise.

16 Find the area of the rectangle.

17 What is the number of interior angles of a rectangle?

18 What is the chance of selecting a card with 1, 2 or 3?

1 2 4 5 3

1 5 4 2 4

19 Write an example of something happening that is unlikely.

20 Complete the Venn diagram to show that 3 people like only cats, 5 people like only dogs and 7 people like both cats and dogs.

cats dogs

21 What was the population in 1990?

22 When was the greatest growth in population?

Population (millions)

Year

UNIT 27A

1

+	4.5	8.1	7.3	4.7	1.5	3.9
2.1						

2

–	4	6.8	7.2	9.1	4.9	8.6
1.5						

3

×	1	7	3	12	9	5
12						

4

×	4	10	2	8	11	6
6						

5

÷	36	84	120	48	132	72
12						

6

÷	90	27	99	36	108	81
9						

7 Find the missing numbers.

```
    3  2  □  8
+   4  □  6  □
--------------
 □  0  1  1
```

8 What is the total of the 3 numbers?

2369 2146 3607

9 Find the difference between 222 798 and 18 640.

10 There were 2793 apples in a warehouse. 1276 were sold. How many apples are left in the warehouse?

11

```
  639
×   7
```

12 Find the total of 9000 × 6.

13

$10\overline{)3640}$

14 Find the missing number.

$$\begin{array}{r} 1240 \\ 6\overline{)} \end{array}$$

15 Find the total of $7^2 - 3^2$.

16 What is 7 °C less than the temperature shown?

–30 –20 –10 0 10 20 30 °C

17 The jacket has been reduced by 50%. What is the new price of the jacket?

Sale price:

Original price: $180

18 Round each to the nearest 5c.

$4116.93 □ $9121.48 □

19 Label the missing value on the number line.

8.1 8.9

20 Find 15.9 ÷ 10.

21 Round each motorbike price to the nearest $1000.

$52 107 $19 299

22 Find the missing numbers.

2 × □ = 240 = □ × 3

UNIT 27B

1 Add the numbers on the cards together to find the total.

38 471 | 29 463 | 10 842

2 What is 5095 less than 83 604?

3 $47\,117 \times 7 =$

4 James sorted 8424 lollies into bags of 9 lollies. How many bags are there?

5 Complete the table.

Decimal	Fraction	Percentage
	$\frac{4}{5}$	
0.2		
		30%

6 Complete with <, > or =.

$\frac{3}{4}$ ☐ $\frac{2}{8}$

7 $4 + (3 \times 7) - 19 =$

8 A musical performance starts at 7:00 pm. It goes for 180 minutes. What time does the musical performance finish?

9 How long did art class go for?

Start time

3:30

End time

10 Find the total amount.

615 g 1.7 kg 0.5 kg

11 Find the area and perimeter of the shape.

8 cm

5 cm

A = P =

12 There are 10 cubes in the base layer of a rectangular prism. If there are 4 layers in the prism, what is the volume of the rectangular prism? cm^3

13 What three-dimensional shape does this net form?

14 Draw the front view of the shape.

side

15 Rotate $\frac{1}{4}$ turn anticlockwise.

16 Find the area of the rectangle.

17 What is the number of interior angles of a regular pentagon?

18 What is the chance of selecting a card with 4 or 5?

1 2 4 5 3

1 5 4 2 4

19 Write an example of something happening that is certain.

20 Complete the Venn diagram to show that 6 people like only bikes, 9 people like only skateboards and 4 people like both bikes and skateboards.

bikes skateboards

21 What was the temperature at 3 pm?

22 What was the temperature drop between 4 pm and 5 pm?

Temp (°C)

Time

2 pm 3 pm 4 pm 5 pm 6 pm

1

+	4.3	2.1	6.9	1.8	3.7	5.2
3.6						

2

–	4	5.6	3.9	7.6	6.7	5.5
1.7						

3

×	4	6	9	2	10	11
12						

4

×	3	8	1	7	12	5
7						

5

÷	84	120	36	72	60	96
12						

6

÷	80	16	32	64	8	96
8						

7 Find the missing numbers.

```
    6  9  □  4
+   2  □  3  □
--------------
    □  7  5  0
```

8 What is the total of the 3 numbers?

5693 1176 3439

9 Find the difference between 718 361 and 24 290.

10 There were 2974 pins in the sewing shop. 1321 were sold. How many pins are left at the shop?

11

$$\begin{array}{r} 721 \\ \times \quad 4 \\ \hline \end{array}$$

12 Find the total of 8000×7.

13

$$10\overline{)6850}$$

14 Find the missing number.

$$\begin{array}{r} 3621 \\ 3\overline{)} \end{array}$$

15 Find the total of $5^2 + 4^2$.

16 What is 3 °C more than the temperature shown?

–30 –20 –10 0 10 20 30 °C

17 The book has been reduced in price by 50%. What is the new price of the book?

Sale price:

Original price: $32.50

18 Round each to the nearest 5c.

$666.27 □ $8919.89 □

19 Label the missing value on the number line.

8.8 9.0

20 Find $79.8 \div 10$.

21 Round each boat price to the nearest $1000.

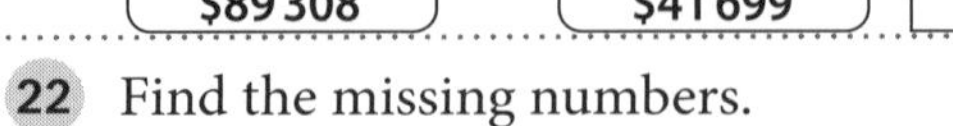

22 Find the missing numbers.

$10 \times \square = 400 = \square \times 8$

UNIT 28B

1 Add the numbers on the cards together to find the total.

68 314 | 72 845 | 11 063

2 What is 3463 less than 69 081?

3 $23\,601 \times 3 =$

4 Sophia sorted 4306 sandwiches into packs of 4. How many whole packs are there?

5 Complete the table.

Decimal	Fraction	Percentage
0.8		
		15%
	$\frac{1}{4}$	

6 Complete with <, > or =.

$\frac{3}{10}$ ☐ $\frac{4}{5}$

7 $(40 \times 3) + (20 \times 4) =$

8 A singing competition starts at 4:45 pm. It goes for 90 minutes. What time does the singing competition finish?

9 How long did sport class go for?

Start time

12:50

End time

10 Find the total amount.

0.9 kg 1.3 kg 600 g

11 Find the area and perimeter of the shape.

A =

P =

8 cm 17 cm 15 cm

12 There are 8 cubes in the base layer of a rectangular prism. If there are 5 layers in the prism, what is the volume of the rectangular prism? ☐ cm^3

13 What three-dimensional shape does this net form?

14 Draw the front view of the shape.

side

15 Rotate [shape] $\frac{1}{4}$ turn anticlockwise.

16 Find the area of the rectangle.

17 What is the number of interior angles of a regular hexagon?

18 What is the chance of selecting a card with a 5?

1 2 4 5 3

1 5 4 2 4

19 Write an example of something happening that is impossible.

20 Complete the Venn diagram to show that 5 people like only pineapple, 10 people like only watermelon and 4 people like both pineapple and watermelon.

pineapple watermelon

21 What was the height of the tree at the third month?

22 How much did the tree grow between the first and second months?

Height of tree (m) 1.0 1.2 1.4 1.6 1.8

Months 1 2 3 4

UNIT
29A

1

+	6.9	8.5	3.6	2.5	8.1	5.2
4.7						

2

–	3.4	5	7.3	9.1	6.9	4.8
1.8						

3

×	1	4	10	7	12	3
12						

4

×	5	9	11	8	2	6
5						

5

÷	120	12	48	108	36	144
12						

6

÷	10	60	90	50	70	100
10						

7 Find the missing numbers.

```
  2 □ 1 7
+ □ 9 3 □
---------
  7 8 □ 6
```

8 What is the total of the 3 numbers?

6931 8576 2117

9 Find the difference between 67 621 and 118 371.

10 There were 2896 flowers at a market stall. 1537 were sold. How many flowers are left?

11

$$\begin{array}{r} 326 \\ \times \quad 7 \\ \hline \end{array}$$

12 Find the total of 6000 × 5.

13

$$10\overline{)7980}$$

14 Find the missing number.

$$\begin{array}{r} 8463 \\ 2\overline{)\quad\quad} \end{array}$$

15 Find the total of $10^2 - 3^2$.

16 What is 8 °C more than the temperature shown?

–30 –20 –10 0 10 20 30 °C

17 The basketball has been reduced in price by 50%. What is the new price of the basketball?

Sale price:

Original price: $48.90

18 Round each to the nearest 5c.

$6121.83 □ $72 120.66 □

19 Label the missing value on the number line.

11 11.2 11.4 11.6 11.8 12

20 Find 164.9 ÷ 10.

21 Round each racing bike price to the nearest $1000.

$1687 $4301

22 Find the missing numbers.

$5 \times \square = 600 = 3 \times \square$

UNIT 29B

1 Add the numbers on the cards together to find the total.

73 281 | 11 634 | 40 685

2 What is 5561 less than 79 381?

3 $42\,110 \times 5 =$

4 Tam sorts 1428 seedlings into tubs of 6. How many tubs are there?

5 Complete the table.

Decimal	Fraction	Percentage
		20%
	$\frac{4}{10}$	
0.17		

6 Complete with <, > or =.

$\frac{2}{3}$ ☐ $\frac{3}{4}$

7 $100 - (3 \times 6) + 5 =$

8 A football match starts at 2:10 pm. It goes for 200 minutes. What time does the football match finish?

9 How long did the talk at the zoo go for?

10:30 Start time

End time

10 Find the total amount.

1.2 kg 400 g $\frac{1}{2}$ kg

11 Find the area and perimeter of the shape.

A =

P =

10 cm

6 cm

12 There are 12 cubes in the base layer of a rectangular prism. If there are 3 layers in the prism, what is the volume of the rectangular prism? ☐ cm^3

13 What three-dimensional shape does this net form?

14 Draw the front view of the shape.

side

15 Reflect the shape horizontally.

16 Find the area of the rectangle.

17 What is the number of interior angles of a trapezium?

18 What is the chance of selecting a card with a 6?

1 | 2 | 4 | 5 | 3
1 | 5 | 4 | 2 | 4

19 Write an example of something that has an equal chance of happening.

20 Complete the Venn diagram to show that 5 people have only a phone, 9 people have only a tablet device and 17 people have both a phone and tablet device.

phone tablet

21 What was the amount of profit at Year 5?

22 What was the decrease in profit between Years 3 and 4?

Profit ($): 10 000, 20 000, 30 000, 40 000, 50 000

Year: 1980, 1990, 2000, 2010, 2020

UNIT 30A

1

+	1.7	6.3	9.8	2.6	4.4	5.5
3.6						

2

–	3	4.6	5.1	7.9	9.4	6.8
1.9						

3

×	1	9	5	11	7	2
12						

4

×	6	10	3	12	8	4
6						

5

÷	120	96	36	12	84	144
12						

6

÷	36	21	27	15	9	30
3						

7 Find the missing numbers.

```
    8 9 1 □
+   2 □ 3 8
-----------
□ □ 5 □ 2
```

8 What is the total of the 3 numbers?

2176 8931 2479

9 Find the difference between 266 824 and 13 872.

10 There are 4972 books in a library. 2532 are borrowed. How many books are left?

11

```
  527
×   4
```

12 Find the total of 9000 × 4.

13

$10\overline{)6930}$

14 Find the missing number.

$$\frac{6931}{2)}$$

15 Find the total of $3^2 + 4^2$.

16 What is 5 °C less than the temperature shown?

–30 –20 –10 0 10 20 30 °C

17 The phone has been reduced in price by 50%. What is the new price of the phone?

Sale price:

Original price: $1320

18 Round each to the nearest 5c.

$4190.72 $63 235.87

19 Label the missing value on the number line.

9.5 9.6 9.7 9.8

20 Find 389.2 ÷ 10.

21 Round each laptop price to the nearest $1000.

$4308 $9147

22 Find the missing numbers.

$6 \times \square = 480 = \square \times 12$

UNIT 30B

1 Add the numbers on the cards together to find the total.

32 110 | 46 109 | 27 998

2 What is 83 291 less than 100 500?

3 $47\,631 \times 7 =$

4 Jacob sorts 1400 flowers into bunches of 8 flowers. How many bunches are there?

5 Complete the table.

Decimal	Fraction	Percentage
1.5		
	$\frac{2}{5}$	
		70%

6 Complete with <, > or =.

$\frac{3}{5}$ ☐ $\frac{2}{3}$

7 $90 + (2 \times 10) + 6 =$

8 A presentation ceremony starts at 6:45 pm. It goes for 90 minutes. What time does the presentation ceremony finish?

9 How long did the talk at the science centre go for?

9:15

Start time

End time

10 Find the total amount.

5200 g $\frac{1}{4}$ kg 3.2 kg

11 Find the area and perimeter of the shape.

A =

P =

3 cm
5 cm
4 cm

12 There are 7 cubes in the base layer of a rectangular prism. If there are 4 layers in the prism, what is the volume of the rectangular prism? ☐ cm^3

13 What three-dimensional shape does this net form?

14 Draw the front view of the shape.

side

15 Reflect the shape vertically down.

16 Find the area of the rectangle.

17 What is the number of interior angles of a parallelogram?

18 What is the chance of selecting a card with an odd number?

1 | 2 | 4 | 5 | 3
1 | 5 | 4 | 2 | 4

19 Write an example of something unlikely happening.

20 Complete the Venn diagram to show that 6 people had only dessert, 8 people had only an entree and 11 people had both an entree and dessert.

entree
dessert

21 How far did the car travel from the start to the end of the first hour?

22 How far did the car travel from hour 2 to hour 3?

Distance (km)
200
150
100
50
1 2 3 4
Time (hrs)

1

+	4.1	7.3	6.4	2.5	5.7	3.9
3.2						

2

–	4.0	5.6	7.2	3.9	2.7	6.1
1.6						

3

×	4	8	1	9	11	3
12						

4

×	6	10	2	5	12	7
5						

5

÷	144	12	72	60	24	120
12						

6

÷	8	32	80	40	88	96
8						

7 Find the missing numbers.

```
    3 [ ] 6  5
+   1  4  7 [ ]
---------------
    5  4 [ ] 4
```

8 Find the total of the numbers on the 3 cards.

3792 4685 5308

[ ]

9

```
  963 114 m
–  24 589 m
```

10 There were 3726 plants at the nursery until 2398 were sold. How many plants were left?

[ ]

11

```
  963
×   5
```

12

$5 \times \square = \square = 4 \times 10$

13

$10\overline{)3980}$

A 398 **B** 39.8
C 39 **D** 39 r8

14 Eight soccer players shared 50 oranges. How many did they each get?

[ ]

15 What is the total of $3^2 + 5^2$?

A 64 **B** 25
C 8 **D** 34

16 How many thousands are in 249 321?

[ ]

17 The hat has been reduced in price by 50%. What is the sale price of the hat?

Sale price: [ ]

Original price: $26

18 What is the difference between $733.98 and $904.66?

[ ]

19 Find 15.3 ÷ 9.

[ ]

20 There are 6 belts. Each belt is 2.1 m long. What is the total length of the belts?

[ ]

21 Round 69 089 107 to the nearest hundred.

[ ]

22 Find the missing number.

$810 + \square = 1140$

1 What is the total of the 3 numbers?

40 000 | 80 000 | 70 000

2 What is 38 496 less than 72 365?

3

$74281 \times 6 =$ ☐

4 Emily sorted 5112 pencils into packets of 9. How many packets were needed altogether?

5 Complete the table.

Decimal	Fraction	Percentage
0.6		
	$\frac{1}{5}$	
		10%

6 Complete with >, < or =.

$\frac{2}{3}$ ☐ $\frac{6}{12}$

7

$(4 \times 9) - (3 \times 7) =$ ☐

8 A show starts at 8:40 pm and goes for 180 minutes. What time does the show finish?

9 How long did sport go for?

Start time | End time 11:15

10 Which is the shortest length?

A 54 cm **B** 5.4 m

C 54 mm **D** 0.5 m

11 Which shape has the greatest area?

A 5 cm, 5 cm **B** 4 cm, 6 cm

12 There are 9 cubes in the base layer of a cube. If there are 3 layers in the cube, what is the volume of the cube? ☐ cm^3

13 What three-dimensional shape does this net form?

14 List all the different shapes of the faces of a triangular-based pyramid.

15 Rotate F one-quarter of a turn anticlockwise.

16 What is the area of the rectangle?

17 What is the number of interior angles of a rhombus?

A 1 **B** 2

C 4 **D** 6

18 What is the chance of selecting a card with a 1 or 6?

1 6 3 5 6

1 1 4 2 4

19 Chase conducted a survey of 50 people to find their favourite sport Use the information to predict how many people in each 1000 would prefer surfing.

Kneeboarding	20
Surfing	13
Waterskiing	5
Beach volleyball	10
Other	2

20 Complete the Venn diagram to show that 9 people like only basketball, 6 people like only soccer and 10 people like both basketball and soccer.

21 What was the temperature drop between 4 pm and 10 pm?

22 What was the number of yellow selected?

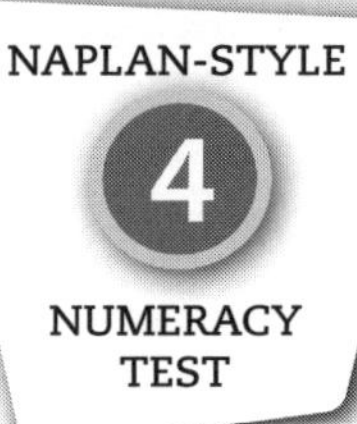

1 What is the total of the numbers on the 3 cards?

6478	3250	1107

A 7585
B 9728
C 10 725
D 10 835

---

2 A farmer has 3890 sheep. He sells 2498 of the sheep. How many sheep does he have left?

A 1392
B 1408
C 1492
D 5188

3

$$\begin{array}{r} 793 \\ \times \quad 8 \\ \hline \end{array}$$

4

$$10\overline{)4786}$$

A 478.6
B 478
C 47.86
D 4786

---

5 What is the total of 3 and 8 each squared and then added together?

A 11
B 55
C 63
D 73

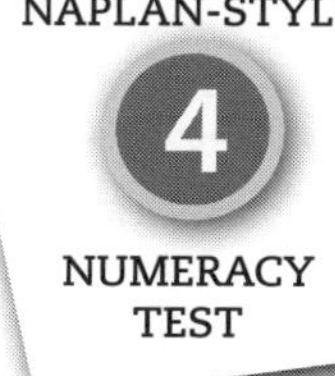

6 The shoes have been reduced to 25% of the original price.
What is the sale price of the shoes?

Sale price: ☐

7 Milly has 6 ribbons. Two of the ribbons are 1.4 m long and 4 of the ribbons are 1.9 m long.
What is the total length of the ribbons?

A 0.5 m
B 2.8 m
C 7.6 m
D 10.4 m

8 What is the missing number?

$$3 \times \square = 6 \times (8 - 2)$$

A 4
B 6
C 12
D 36

9 19.6 divided by 4 equals

A 4
B 4.9
C 5
D 6.2

10 Heath rounded 4 172 307 to the nearest hundred. What did Heath write?

A 4 172 000
B 4 172 300
C 4 172 400
D 4 173 000

11 The distance between Melbourne and Sydney is 878.2 km. The distance between Melbourne and Perth is 3406.4 km. What is the difference between the two distances?

A 2528.2 km
B 3272.2 km
C 3472.2 km
D 4284.6 km

12 There are 3274 drawing pins in every box. The bookshop has 5 boxes of drawing pins. How many drawing pins do they have altogether?

☐

13 Complete the table.

Decimal	Fraction	Percentage
0.06		

14 The movie starts at 11.20 am. The length of the movie is 190 minutes. What time does the movie finish?

A 1:10 pm
B 1:40 pm
C 2:00 pm
D 2:30 pm

15 Complete with < , > or =.

$$\frac{3}{8} \;\square\; \frac{2}{3}$$

16 Julie wants the piece of paper with the greatest area. Which one does she pick?

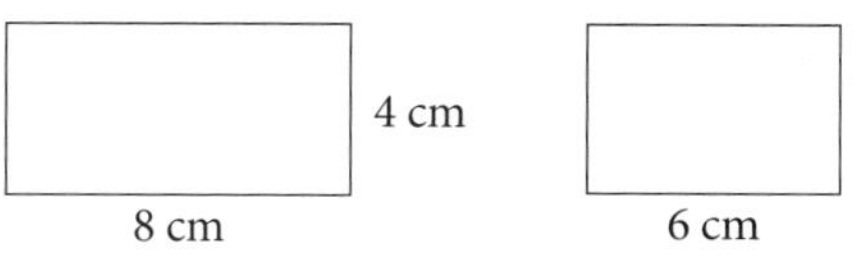

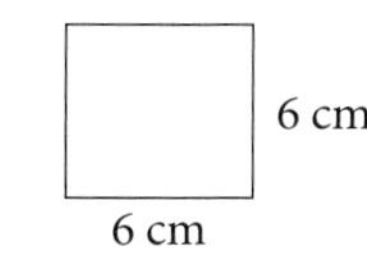

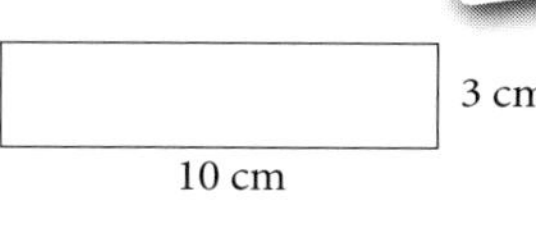

A **B** **C** **D**

---

17 In a box, 100 centimetre-cubes fill the base. There are 10 layers of cubes in the box. What is the volume of the box?

A 100 cm^3
B 110 cm^3
C 1000 cm^3
D 10 000 cm^3

---

18 Gary rotates the letter M one quarter turn anticlockwise. What does Gary draw?

A

B

C

D

---

19 What is the perimeter of the rectangle on the coordinate axes?

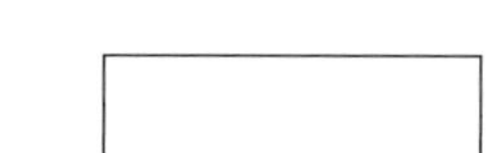

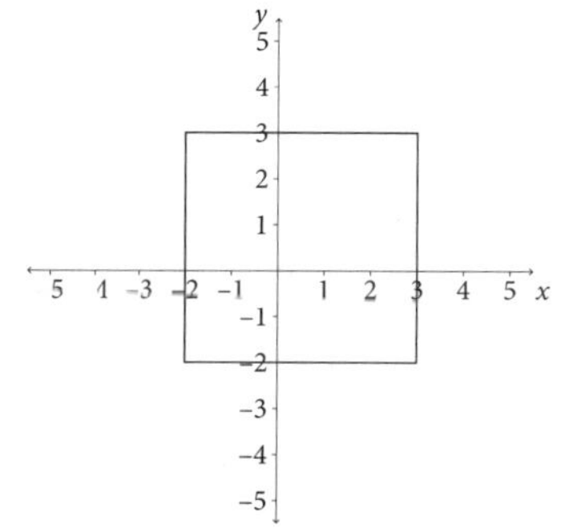

---

20 Mum left her coffee on the bench. Stu measured the temperature. After how many minutes was the coffee 80 °C?

A 0
B 2 min
C 3 min
D 4 min

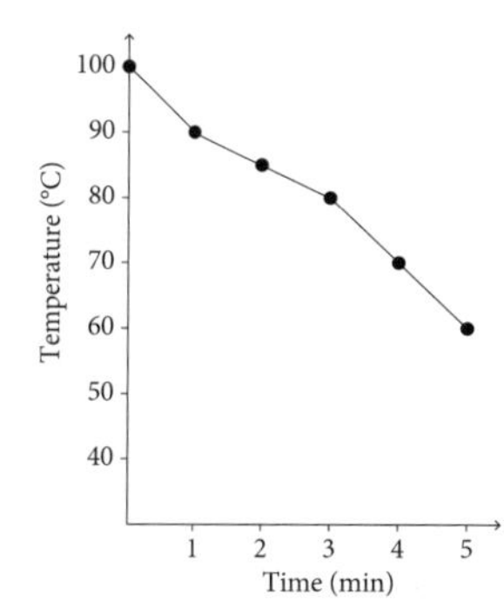

Reprinted 2020, 2021, 2022

Updated in 2023 for the NSW Curriculum and Australian Curriculum Version 9.0 changes

Reprinted 2024

ISBN 978 1 74125 621 5

Pascal Press
PO Box 250
Glebe NSW 2037
(02) 9198 1748
www.pascalpress.com.au

Publisher: Vivienne Joannou
Project editor: Rosemary Peers
Edited by Rosemary Peers
Answers checked by Peter Little and Melinda Amaral
Page design by Kim Webber
Typeset by lj Design (Julianne Billington) and Grizzly Graphics (Leanne Richters)
Printed by Vivar Printing/Green Giant Press

The publisher thanks the Royal Australian Mint for granting permission to use Australian currency coin designs in this book.